The Person in Social Psychology

- Vivien Burr

First published 2002
by Psychology Press Ltd
27 Church Road, Hove,
East Sussex BN3 2FA
www.psypress.co.uk

Simultaneously published in
the USA and Canada
by Taylor & Francis, Inc.
29 West 35th Street,
New York NY 10001

Psychology Press is part of the Taylor & Francis Group

© 2002 Vivien Burr

Cover design and illustration by
Terry Foley

Typeset in Sabon and Futura by
Florence Production Ltd, Stoodleigh,
Devon
Printed and bound in Great Britain
by TJ International Ltd,
Padstow, Cornwall

*British Library Cataloguing in
Publication Data*
A catalogue record for this book is
available from the British Library

*Library of Congress Cataloging-in-
Publication Data*
Burr, Vivien.
  The person in social psychology/
Vivien Burr.
    p. cm – (Psychology focus)
  Includes bibliographical references
and index.
  ISBN 1–84169–180–1 (hc)—
  ISBN 1–84169–181–X (pbk)
  1. Social Psychology. 2. Human
Behaviour. 3. Social role –
Psychological aspects. 4. Social
groups – Psychological aspects.
  I. Title. II. Series
  HM1033.b87 2002
302—dc21   2001044215

ISBN 1–84169–181–X (pbk)
ISBN 1–84169–180–1 (hbk)

Contents

CONTENTS

Series preface

The Psychology Focus series provides short, up-to-date accounts of key areas in psychology without assuming the reader's prior knowledge in the subject. Psychology is often a favoured subject area for study, since it is relevant to a wide range of disciplines such as Sociology, Education, Nursing and Business Studies. These relatively inexpensive but focused short texts combine sufficient detail for psychology specialists with sufficient clarity for non-specialists.

The series authors are academics experienced in undergraduate teaching as well as research. Each takes a topic within their area of psychological expertise and presents a short review, highlighting important themes and including both theory and research findings. Each aspect of the topic is clearly explained with supporting glossaries to elucidate technical terms.

The series has been conceived within the context of the increasing modularisation which has been developed in higher education over the last decade and fulfils the consequent need for clear, focused, topic-based course material. Instead of following one course of study, students on a modularisation programme are often able to choose modules from a wide range of disciplines to complement the modules they are required to study for a specific degree. It can no longer be assumed that students studying a particular module will necessarily have the same background knowledge (or lack of it!) in that subject. But they will need to familiarise themselves with a particular topic rapidly since a single module in a single topic may be only 15 weeks long, with assessments arising during that period. They may have to combine eight or more modules in a single year to obtain a degree at the end of their programme of study.

One possible problem with studying a range of separate modules is that the relevance of a particular topic or the relationship between topics may not always be apparent. In the Psychology Focus series, authors have drawn where possible on practical and applied examples to support the points being made so that readers can see the wider relevance of the topic under study. Also, the study of psychology is usually broken up into separate areas, such as social psychology, developmental psychology and cognitive psychology, to take three examples. Whilst the books in the Psychology Focus series will provide excellent coverage of certain key topics within these 'traditional' areas, the authors have not been constrained in their examples and explanations and may draw on material across the whole field of psychology to help explain the topic under study more fully.

Each text in the series provides the reader with a range of important material on a specific topic. They are suitably comprehensive and give a clear account of the important issues involved. The authors analyse and interpret the material as well as present an up-to-date and detailed review of key work. Recent references are provided along with suggested further reading to allow readers to investigate the topic in more depth. It is hoped, therefore, that after following the informative review of a key topic in a Psychology Focus text, readers not only will have a clear understanding of the issues in question but will be intrigued and challenged to investigate the topic further.

Acknowledgements

I am indebted to Viv Ward and Perry Hinton for their time and patience in helping me to think through the idea for this book, and to colleagues for giving me the time and opportunity to write it. Once more I am most grateful to the ever-reliable Geoff Adams for his preparation of the index.

Chapter 1

The individual and the social in social psychology

The aims of this book

PSYCHOLOGY IS ALL ABOUT trying to understand people's behaviour and experiences. It constantly asks what human nature is. It asks 'what is it to be a person?'. It then attempts to offer some answers to our questions about why people do, say and feel the things they do. But if you are a student of psychology, you will quickly learn that the discipline does not offer a single answer to this question. In fact different branches of psychology offer us quite different accounts of human behaviour and experience. For trait theorists like Eysenck and Cattell, our behaviour and experience is the outcome of personality characteristics that are 'hard-wired', passed down to us through genetic inheritance. For psychodynamic theorists like Freud, Klein and Winnicott the key to understanding humanity is not in traits but in age-old and unavoidable conflicts played out between parents and children in early life. For behaviourists like Watson, Skinner and Thorndike the answer is different again; we are understood here as essentially adaptable animals that learn from their experiences, so we are products of environmental events that shape and determine our behaviour. Humanistic psychologists, like Malsow and Rogers, see us as unique individuals, each one having an innate potential that we can fulfil if we are allowed to develop properly. The differences between these approaches are not just academic. They have implications for how we can and should live our lives, and for how much power we have to change ourselves and our society. An important part of our job as psychologists is therefore evaluating these perspectives, asking ourselves whether the images of humanity they present are accurate or misleading, useful or constraining, helpful or downright dangerous.

As social psychologists our task must therefore be the same. We have to look behind the theories and research that have made up this sub-discipline of psychology over approximately the last 100 years and ask ourselves what kind of persons we are and can be according to its accounts. And, just as with its parent discipline, social psychology has more than one answer to the question. Our task must be to take a close and critical look at these accounts in order to find out whether we like the look of the person lurking behind them. This isn't always a simple matter, because sometimes the nature of this person is present by implication rather than explicitly stated. Students therefore often find that, although they become familiar with the subject matter of social psychology, they don't see the bigger picture of the person that exists between the lines of the text book. The aim of this book is to make this person (or persons!) more visible and therefore more open to critical scrutiny.

When I was a psychology undergraduate in the 1970s it was relatively unusual for students to learn much about the historical and philosophical influences that had shaped their discipline. I think this is a great shame, as a whole generation of academic psychologists were left without some important intellectual tools with which to reflect upon and properly critique their own and others' work. If we want to get to know someone properly, to understand how and why they see things as they do, we try to find out something about their personal history, their early life, the kind of environment they grew up in, their hopes and aspirations. In the same way, in order to understand properly the nature of the persons implicated in these social psychologies, we must know something about their history, where and why they emerged, and how the traces of their early lives can still be seen today.

However, it wouldn't be fair to say that this is going to be an impartial account. In scrutinising the different varieties of social psychology I shall certainly be offering some comment on their strengths and weaknesses. But there is also a strong sense in which this book will be advocating a particular position throughout, and this is the view that the person is a fundamentally social phenomenon. This is a view that is consistent with several of the social psychologies covered here, so I am not advocating any particular theory but rather contrasting the different approaches to social psychology in terms of the extent to which they see the person as a social being. In effect, this will take the form of a challenge to a social psychology that analyses social phenomena at the level of the minds and behaviour of individuals. This includes much of what is usually referred to as conventional North American social psychology. It will on the other hand entail an advocacy of newer social psychologies originating in Europe (and to a lesser extent North America) as well as more sociological (but not necessarily newer) North American social psychologies.

A great deal of what is taught on undergraduate social psychology modules consists of theories and research originating in North America in the early and mid-twentieth century and being further developed today. I will therefore begin by tracing something of the history of the person in this account. I will show how this profile of the person as sketched by academic social psychologists shares many of the same features of the person as implicitly understood by ordinary people living in Western industrialised countries over the last three hundred years. We will see that we can recognise these assumptions about what it means to be a person if we look closely at the theories and research within this social psychology. The chapter will conclude by sketching the outline of a different kind of *social* person, one that is perhaps not as easily recognisable to us as yet.

The roots of the modern individual

It is no surprise that the historical and philosophical influences that shaped psychology were passed on to social psychology as it began to take shape as a body of theory and research. What were these influences, and how do we recognise them in our understanding of personhood today? People in contemporary Western societies share a common idea of what being a person entails, even though we do not often articulate this idea to ourselves and others.

Although we might agree that we all share a common humanity and therefore have common needs and perhaps even common human rights, we also think of people as unique individuals, each with their own abilities, talents, characters and preferences. Whether these are innate or acquired, it is this unique set of characteristics that makes us who we are and we often use these characteristics to explain why people behave and feel the way they do. Furthermore, these characteristics are thought of as relatively stable or consistent, so that we think of ourselves as being the same person from day to day, from week to week, and even from year to year. And our personality is thought to be coherent in the sense that we do not normally feel ourselves to be a random mixture of incompatible or inconsistent attributes. We certainly recognise inner conflicts, and can feel pulled in different directions by different sides of our nature, but this is experienced as a problem and one that needs resolving back into coherence. We see our actions as the outcome of rational deliberation and decision-making – at least we feel that it *ought* to be so. We generally see our conduct as the outcome of freely chosen courses of action. We set great store by this freedom to do as we see fit, and, since we must bear responsibility for our actions, we are prepared to publicly defend them as rational, logical and morally legitimate ones. We applaud and respect those who steadfastly refuse to waver from their beliefs in the face of coercion or propaganda, and criticise those who unthinkingly adopt the behaviour and attitudes of their peers. This is not simply a description of the contemporary individual, it is an ideal to which we feel we must aspire. We place great value upon it.

However, such a vision of humanity is a fairly recent acquisition in the history of Western civilisation. The threads woven into the contemporary individual can be traced back to developments in knowledge, thinking, religion and technology over the last few hundred years. They can be seen emerging at the end of the Middle Ages, at the start of what is known as the Renaissance, around the fourteenth century. The Renaissance period, which flourished in Western Europe until about the seventeenth century, encouraged the extension of the boundaries of learning and geographical knowledge, and saw the proliferation of scientists and explorers. It also encouraged scepticism and free thought. The religious dogma of the Middle Ages had emphasised blind obedience to the dictates of religious leaders. The new scepticism of the Renaissance challenged this, encouraging people to form their own individual opinions and beliefs. With the Reformation of the sixteenth century, the political power of the papacy was challenged. Farr (1996) describes how technological advances at the time led to the rise of the modern individual and its prevalence in North American thinking:

> The invention of the printing press and the spread of literacy further promoted [individualism] by producing active minorities who could read holy writ for themselves rather than accept the word of others, who protested at the propaganda, who dissented from the former consensus, and who failed, generally, to conform. The spokesmen (for they were men) for the pious majority represented these deviants as Protestants, Dissenters and Nonconformists. Once the representation had been formed, individuals could be identified and then persecuted. Persecution in the Old World led to selective

migration to the New. This, in turn, led to individualism being a more central value in North America than, say, in Central Europe.

(p. 103)

But the real explosion in scientific activity and free-thinking came in the period following the Renaissance, known as the Enlightenment, which reached its peak in the eighteenth century. The Enlightenment was a European intellectual movement. Enlightenment thinkers believed in the liberating possibilities of rational and scientific knowledge. They were often critical of existing society, and believed in the possibility of progress. They were hostile to religion, which they saw as keeping the human mind chained down by superstition. Science was seen as the enlightened alternative to the religious dogma of earlier times. The truth about the world was now seen not as delivered ready-made by the dictates of religious leaders, but as discoverable by free-thinking human beings through their scientific endeavours. It was now up to individuals to find out the truth for themselves.

Enlightenment thinking was characterised by the idea that we can discover the principles governing nature by applying rational analysis and scientific method. For example, Sir Isaac Newton laid down a very few laws that could describe and predict events in the natural world very accurately, such as the movement of the celestial bodies. It was anticipated that we could eventually bring events in the world under our control through the understanding and predictive power offered by science. Scientists like Newton had had considerable success in explaining things that had previously been inexplicable and in generating useful technology, so confidence grew in the belief that science would eventually be able to find the answers to all our questions. In this period, impressive machines had been invented for various purposes. The world, including the realm of human events, was seen as a complex machine that operated under orderly, mechanistic laws and principles, just like clocks or engines, and it was expected that we could eventually, by scientific method, come to understand these laws and make predictions from them. The metaphor of things as machines is as much at the root of psychology today as it was in its infancy. Today's cognitive science has the computer as its metaphor for psychological phenomena, just as in the past Freud saw the psyche as operating like a hydraulic system, and the early behaviourists saw the mechanism of the reflex arc as the fundamental principle of human behaviour.

The seventeenth-century philosopher Descartes was an important figure in shaping our modern notion of the individual. Descartes' use of 'methodological doubt', by which he pressed himself to question all of his pre-existing beliefs and knowledge in the search for facts of which he could be certain, led him to a theoretical position that is known as dualism. This is the view that the world consists of two different kinds of things, those that are pure thought, which are subjective and internal to the person, and those that are objective, external to the person and material in nature. Even the body was seen by him as constituting part of the external (to the self), material world, and he regarded the person as an entirely mental and subjective phenomenon. He thought this because we can conceive of ourselves as existing without bodies, but cannot conceive of ourselves as existing without conscious awareness. This 'Cartesian dualism' therefore splits the mind from the body and locates all the important features of being a person clearly in the mental realm. It separates the subjective from the objective world, so that the person becomes an in-dwelling (or intra-psychic) being that receives and interprets information about its environment, and that environment includes other people. But how was it possible for the mind to move the body and manipulate external objects, thus bringing about effects in the material world? Descartes did not come up with a convincing account of how the mind and the body could influence each other, and it is interesting to reflect that psychology today, despite decades of research on brain structures, hormones and genetic material, still struggles with this question of the relationship between mind and body.

We can now begin to see how we have come to our current notion of the person as a free-thinking moral agent with its own unique thoughts, beliefs and values, an individual contained within its own psychological space, separated from material reality and from other individuals. Looked at in this historical context, our modern notion of what it means to be a person has not substantially changed in important respects in over two hundred years. But we must nevertheless remember that this way of thinking did not characterise earlier historical epochs and is characteristic of only some societies today. Farr (1996) goes to the extent of referring to this individualism as an ideology, in order to show both its dependency upon time and place and its power to influence our thinking:

> When individualism becomes a dominant ideology within a culture, it is no longer visible to those whose ideology it is. Indeed, they often write books celebrating the end of ideology ... They equate ideology with collective beliefs ... When the object of these collective beliefs is the individual, this is not thought to be an ideology – rather, it is thought to be the antithesis of ideology.
>
> (p. 104)

Psychology and the individual

Within this individualist view the social context, consisting of other people, in which a person lives may impinge upon or influence him or her, but this influence is seen as being exerted upon a person that pre-exists and is independent of that social context. The characteristics of a person could therefore, at least in principle, be described once and for all, since the nature of the person is seen as not dependent upon social context. We can see that the discipline of psychology bears the trademarks of its historical and philosophical roots. One could even say that psychology is an axiomatic example of the individualism documented above. Its subject area is the mental life and behaviour of individuals. Just as it was for Descartes, the body is seen as a vehicle for the mind and psychology's interest in the body has been to enquire after the physiological correlates of mental events and to ask whether our psychology can be reduced to them. Psychology's explicit aim in its experimental tradition has been to discover the character-istics of individuals in their pure form, uncontaminated by extraneous variables in the external, material and social world beyond the laboratory. It has adopted the philosophy and the methods of the natural sciences, and, like the early scientists of the Enlightenment, has committed itself to discovering the laws and mechanisms underlying events, in this case human events.

But studies of non-Western cultures provide further support for the view that individualism is not a fact of human nature but a product of history, which throws into question the adequacy of such a psychology for understanding peoples less influenced by European and North American philosophy and history. Lalljee (1996) argues that in non-Western societies, such as India and Japan, people are understood primarily in terms of their social roles and relationships rather than their psychological attributes because of the interconnectedness of people's lives in those soci-eties. He cites a number of studies that suggest the prevalence of a more collective or social sense of self in some cultures. For example, in a self-description task Dutch children tended to offer more descriptions of psychological traits and attitudes while Moroccan children referred to social characteristics such as group membership. In another study, self-descriptions of Japanese and North American students were compared. The Japanese students were much less likely to use psychological descriptions (such as 'I am honest') than the North American students, and preferred social role descriptors such as 'college student' and 'father'. Even the nature of insults has been found to vary, with individualist cultures preferring references to personal qualities (for example 'ugly' or 'stupid') and more collectivist cultures making reference to the person's relations with others or their family members.

The point at issue here is a central one for social psychol-ogists. If we want to understand people's actions and their experiences, should we think of people as having a basic nature (this might include both universal characteristics that could be referred to as 'human nature' as well as personality characteris-tics) which then responds in various ways to exposure to all the different social circumstances with which a person's life presents them? Within this way of thinking, we would be drawn to ask questions like 'How are the normal human decision-making processes affected by being a member of a group?' or 'How is our information-processing affected by the characteristics and behaviour of other people when we make social judgements?'. Here, other people and the social situations they constitute for us as participants are seen as events that lead to potentially describable and predictable changes in our normal, individual psychology. To put the extreme case for the sake of argument, you could say that the way to find out what people are *really* like would be to take away all the social variables that affect their everyday behaviour and secretly observe them alone on a desert island.

Sometimes this way of asking questions is quite fruitful. For example, the social facilitation experiments of Triplett (1898) showed that people try harder at a task if other people are present than if they are alone. But sometimes our questions about people can't be posed in this way. If we want to find out, say, how being a Catholic affects one's personality we just can't reduce 'being a Catholic' to a set of variables that can be thought of as impinging upon an already-existing individual. Could you, even in theory, take away the 'Catholic' bits of the person and examine what is left? It doesn't make sense, because everything that is entailed in 'being a Catholic' (from attending mass and confession to marital and sexual relations) is more usefully thought of as part and parcel of who the person *is* rather than a set of variables outside of them. This doesn't mean that we shouldn't ask these questions, but it does mean that we have to look beyond the notion of the individual for our answers. We would have to examine the social practices, family and community relations, shared beliefs and expectations and so on that make up 'being a Catholic'. As we shall see in the next section, social psychology, as it is studied by most psychologists, has for various historical reasons largely followed the former route.

The emergence of social psychology

The term 'social psychology' only really took hold during the twentieth century, and most of the research that today would be recognised as social psychology only began in the 1930s. However, the characteristic concerns of social psychology can be traced back to the second half of the nineteenth century. Then, as today, the issues that writers of the time addressed were those of pressing social problems. The problems of the day arose at the time of and following the Industrial Revolution in Europe. For example, in France revolution and revolt by the masses had led to widespread fear among the ruling classes that society was in decline. Gustav Le Bon (1895) explained crowd behaviour, such as riots, by proposing the existence of a primitive 'crowd mind'. Drawing on the recently developed medical concept of contagion, Le Bon argued that *mental* contagion could account for the spread of emotion and 'anomie' in agitated crowds. Anomie is a condition, so named by Emil Durkheim, the founder of modern sociology, in which social norms are ignored or contested. Crowd psychology was also influenced by criminology, so that the individual under the influence of the crowd was thought to suffer diminished responsibility. Graumann (1988) thus characterises the individual according to this crowd psychology as becoming

> more primitive, more infantile than when alone, and hence less intelligent, less guided by reason and therefore less responsible . . . a major concern of the Latin crowd psychology was the fate of the "normal" individual who became somehow "abnormal" under the social condition of the crowd
>
> (p. 11)

Le Bon's book caused a great deal of debate around the question as to whether a crowd or group could be considered to have a mind, a phenomenon that was more than the sum of the individual minds that comprised the group and that could be analysed and understood in its own terms. At the heart of this debate are two different conceptions of the relationship between the individual and the social. Writers like Le Bon and Durkheim,

11

although they were ultimately interested in explaining the conduct of individual persons, saw such conduct as only understandable through an appreciation of the social context. This social context needed its own special kinds of concepts and explanations (like crowd mind and anomie) and could not be reduced to the sum of or outcome of actions of individuals. The alternative view is that social phenomena (like crowd behaviour) can be understood by examining the psychological processes of individuals. As we shall see, the two different ways of viewing social psychology became theoretically and methodologically divorced from one another, and it is the more individualistic conception of social psychology that took root in Britain and North America.

The simultaneous publication of two books, both called 'Social Psychology' in 1908, symbolises the split between these two different conceptions of social psychology. Although symbolic of the split, neither of these books in themselves exerted a strong influence on the future of social psychology, and indeed Farr (1996) argues that the segregation of these two forms of social psychology could not clearly be seen until after the Second World War. The books were written by William McDougall, a British psychologist, and Edward Ross, a North American sociologist. McDougall was a follower of Le Bon, and later took up and wrote about his group mind idea. Nevertheless, he did view the individual as the proper focus of social psychology. Ross, on the other hand, felt that social psychology should examine phenomena at the level of the collective or social interaction. As psychology and sociology themselves emerged as separate disciplines with different concerns and different methodologies, the social psychologies associated with them became likewise segregated and have continued to live more or less separate lives for most of the twentieth century. We can therefore speak of at least two fundamentally different kinds of social psychology: *psychological* social psychology and *sociological* social psychology.

Psychological social psychology was inevitably shaped by the powerful influence of the individualistic, empiricist and increasingly institutionalised psychology that was gaining ground in North America. Wilhelm Wundt is considered the nineteenth-century founder of psychology as a discipline. He established the first experimental psychology laboratory at Leipzig University in 1879, and is therefore seen as a key figure in the establishment of psychology as a science. However, Wundt believed that psychology could only to a limited extent be regarded as a branch of the natural sciences, and he therefore believed that only some aspects of psychology could appropriately be studied in the laboratory. He believed, for example, that higher mental processes such as thought and memory could not adequately be studied experimentally. His use of the laboratory was to investigate the nature of immediate conscious experiences that a person could report on, such as physical sensations and emotions. It can be a surprise to contemporary psychology students to learn that he was also interested in phenomena that have long since been exiled to neighbouring disciplines such as sociology and anthropology, topics such as religion, myth and social customs – like the example of Catholicism above. So, like Le Bon and Durkheim, he felt that individual behaviour could not be understood without reference to its social context and his psychology was therefore not coloured by an untempered individualist philosophy. During the latter half of the nineteenth century and the first half of the twentieth century, thousands of North Americans went to Europe to study, and on their return to America a few pioneers set up their own laboratories, modelled on that of Wundt in Leipzig. However, in its journey to North America, Wundt's psychology underwent a transformation and the psychology practised in these new laboratories reflected the individualism of North American culture. These laboratories soon established very different research programmes to that of Wundt, for example the investigation of individual differences. Wundt's method of 'introspection' (the reflecting upon and reporting of private mental and sensory events in a systematic way) was heavily criticised by John Watson, one of the founders of behaviourism, and it continues to be seen by today's psychologists as unacceptably subjective and therefore unscientific. So it is fair to say that only part of Wundt's psychology, the focus on studying phenomena in the laboratory, was adopted and developed by North American psychologists.

Nevertheless, Wundt's interest in the relationship between the individual and society was not completely ignored by social scientists. It was taken up by the philosopher George Mead in America. Mead was one of the thousands who had gone to Germany to pursue a graduate education and he was based at the University of Chicago at the turn of the century. Like Wundt he believed that social phenomena could not be understood by appealing only to the psychology of individuals, and devoted himself to analysing the relations between mind and consciousness on the one hand and society on the other. At this time, John Watson was a graduate student at Chicago (he was in fact one of Mead's students) and then became an instructor there. Mead was highly critical of Watson's behaviourism, which appealed to the positivist and empiricist scientific culture in America. This disagreement between Mead and Watson marks the beginning of the split between sociological and psychological forms of social psychology.

Watson, who had studied learning in rats as a PhD student, took the radically empiricist view that psychology should concern itself only with the objective observation of behaviour. In 1913 he published his behaviourist manifesto, in which he pledged to rid psychology of all reference to mind and consciousness. He argued that since we have no direct access to the experience of other people, their consciousness, we are not in a position to study it scientifically. Rather than rely on their verbal reports of their experience, we should limit ourselves to what we can actually witness at first-hand: behaviour. Watson's interest in the principles of learning was well-suited to laboratory study, largely using animals rather than human participants. Skinner later extended the behaviourist approach to learning into the human domain, and the momentum of such laboratory experimentation carried behaviourism well into the twentieth century as a major force in psychology, both in its theory and in its method.

Psychological social psychology

While psychology in Europe was still a matter of largely un-coordinated efforts by individual academics, psychology in North America quickly became stronger and more institutionalised. The psychology of North America thus came to dominate the field, leading to what has been termed the Americanisation of the discipline. Behaviourism, which seemed to offer the possibility of the scientific prediction and control of human events, quickly became dominant. As behaviourism took hold of and defined psychology in the early part of the twentieth century, the discipline became thoroughly individualistic and de-contextualised. Mind and culture, which had been of such interest to the early European psychologists and to Mead, were no longer legitimate subjects of psychological concern. In addition to this, behaviourism established the experiment as the only legitimate form of enquiry for a scientific psychology.

The social psychology practised by psychologists therefore inevitably took on this individualistic and behaviouristic flavour. This is shown in F.H. Allport's (1924) *Social psychology*, which had a formative influence on the discipline and helped to establish social psychology in North America as an experimental and behavioural science. Like Watson, Allport was a behaviourist and rejected the study of mind and consciousness. For Allport, social psychology was 'the science which studies the behavior of the individual in so far as his [*sic*] behavior stimulates other individuals, or is itself a reaction to this behavior' (p. 12) (cited in Hewstone *et al.*, 1988). Allport, like other social psychologists, was certainly interested in explaining collective phenomena. However, the difference between him and writers such as Wundt, Durkheim, Le Bon, Mead and McDougall is that he believed that group phenomena could be explained in terms of individual psychology and that special concepts such as group mind were not necessary. When McDougall published his book *The group mind* in 1920 and moved to America to take up a position at Harvard University, Allport was very critical of his appearing to suggest that entities other than individuals (that is, groups or crowds) could take action or have agency. Allport was therefore instrumental in bringing about what Farr calls the 'individualization of the social' (1996, p. 10) in social psychology.

When Hitler came to power in Germany in 1933, many Jewish academics emigrated to America. Significant among these were the Gestalt psychologists, most notably Kurt Lewin. The Gestalt psychologists differed radically from the behaviourists in two major respects. Firstly, they rejected their atomistic view of the person, arguing that human phenomena are always greater than the sum of their individual parts. Thus, we cannot expect to understand the person adequately through the study of fragmented pieces of behaviour or through reducing a social situation to a set of separate variables. Secondly, they argued that one could only understand a person's conduct through an appreciation of their phenomenal world, through an understanding of their subjective viewpoint rather than an objective record of their behaviour. But it favoured the same experimental methodology as behaviourism, having its roots in the same German experimental tradition that Wundt had earlier initiated in his Leipzig laboratory. As Gestalt psychology became absorbed into North American social psychology it took on that culture's focus upon individual psychology and its practical applications, and Gestalt psychology's earlier concern with subjective experience re-emerged as the study of social cognition.

Research in social psychology over most of the twentieth century can be seen to carry these hallmarks. The questions social psychologists posed themselves were often prompted by social events and problems of considerable concern, such as the blind obedience to authority thought to underlie many Nazi atrocities, the unpreparedness to help others who are in danger, or racial prejudice. Nevertheless, the experimentalism and individualism of social psychology has meant that such questions have often been posed within the narrow confines of the laboratory in terms restricted to the behaviour and thinking of individuals. The studies by Milgram (1963) and by Asch (1956) on obedience to authority and conformity, the work of Latané and Darley (1969) on bystander apathy, and the minimal group experiments of Tajfel et al. (1971) are examples.

Sociological social psychology

George Mead is an important figure in the development of the sociological strand of social psychology, and it is testimony to the segregation of this from the psychological brand that few psychology undergraduates today know much about him or the theory of symbolic interactionism that was developed from his work. When Mead had originally joined the University of Chicago, the department included philosophy, psychology and education. But in 1904 the psychologists formed a separate department. Mead stayed with the philosophers, while Watson joined the psychologists. This was one reason why the burgeoning behaviourist psychology was not informed by philosophy, and it was sociology graduate students at the university who were encouraged to attend Mead's lectures.

Like Wundt before him, Mead felt that language, society and culture were vital to an understanding of human action. But Wundt's conception of mind still followed a Cartesian dualism that separated the knower from the known, the subject from the object, the self from the other. Wundt therefore found it difficult to explain the relationship between individual and society. Mead's contribution lies in transcending these dualisms, in particular the division between self and other, and in providing an account of the individual that is thoroughly social. His conception of mind and of consciousness, and of the relationship between these and society, was based upon the interdependency of self and other. Furthermore, language and social interaction were for Mead crucial to the development of the mind, consciousness and the self. For Mead, the self does not pre-exist society, it emerges from it. His social psychology is therefore radically different from psychological social psychology, where the individual or self (in those psychologies which accept the existence of a self) is not dependent upon social forces for its existence (although traditional psychology does accept that the individual is to some degree *shaped* by social experience).

Like Watson, Mead was interested in why people behave as they do. But he felt that people's behaviour is always bound up and coordinated with that of the others who form their environment; our behaviour can only therefore be properly understood if we look at it in the context of other people's conduct and the history of their relations with each other. He turns on its head psychology's question of how individual persons, who are conscious and have minds, come to interact with other individuals, affect and be affected by them, so producing something that is called society. Instead, he sees consciousness and mind (our ability to reflect upon our actions and those of others) as the outcomes of social interaction. Mead's individual does not exist independently of society but is instead made possible by social interaction between people. And the key to the development of mind is something distinctly human; our ability to use symbols to represent things and events, especially our use of language. It is language, says Mead, that allows us to internalise social interaction, to represent it to ourselves and to think about and reflect upon it, and this is what mind is. A symbol (such as a word) is something that carries meaning, and that meaning is not something private to solitary individuals: meanings are shared among social groups. So, for example, the words 'I love you', or 'Dreadful weather we're having today' or the symbolic gesture of a candle-lit dinner all have a meaning that is shared in our culture.

These shared meanings have three important implications. First, in opposition to the claims of behaviourism, behaviour is not the outcome of objective events but arises from the symbolic meaning those events have for people. We therefore cannot understand why people behave as they do without looking at their subjective, phenomenal world, as the Gestalt psychologists did. Second, those meanings are specific to particular cultures, so that we cannot assume that our understanding of behaviour in our own culture can simply be applied to people in other cultures or at other times in history. And third, the shared nature of such meanings gives us a way of appreciating the intentions, anticipations and responses of others. It enables us to coordinate our activities in complex and intricate ways, so that our own conduct becomes continually informed by the anticipated conduct of others. Mead calls this 'taking the role of the other'. Because we can imagine the meaning that words and events hold for other people, we are continually stepping in and out of their perspective, their role in events, in forming our own conduct. In this way we come to have a concept of ourselves as others might see us. It is this process that makes it possible for us to be self-aware, to be conscious of *being* a self. Mead called his approach 'social behaviourism', but the theory was later taken up by one of Mead's students, Blumer, who called it 'symbolic interactionism'.

In more recent times, since the Second World War, the focus of interest of symbolic interactionism upon meaning, social interaction and role taking has been taken up in a variety of different ways. For example, Erving Goffman, also working at the University of Chicago, looked at role playing in terms of the scripts governing social interaction. The ethnomethodology developed by Harold Garfinkel focused on the use of language in social interaction, showing how shared assumptions about the situation in which we are interacting with others is vital for our talk to be meaningfully interpreted and understood by them. And Howard Becker, who was influential in the development of labelling theory (see Chapter 4), looked at how deviance could be thought of not as a property of particular individuals, but as a product of social interaction and negotiation, as 'a quality or qualities *imputed* to the person and his or her acts by social classification' (Hewitt, 1988, p. 240, italics in original).

It is clear from this account that the social psychology derived from Mead is not behaviouristic, although it is cognitive in the sense that mental events, the thoughts and ideas that constitute our response to meaning, are crucial to understanding our behaviour. It places social interaction centre-stage and refuses to study the behaviour of individuals in isolation, stripped of its social and historical context. The methods that have typically been used in investigations within sociological social psychology have therefore not included laboratory experimentation but have been those that attempt to access the meanings that are salient to particular pieces of conduct or that allow an analysis of interaction taking place in its natural context, such as interviews and participant observation. For example, Becker (1953) used interviews and symbolic interactionist theory in his study of marihuana use and Goffman (1967) reports how he used observation to examine social rules (regarding propriety) by studying how these are routinely broken by mental patients.

The crisis in social psychology and recent developments

By the late 1960s and early 1970s, psychological social psychology had developed well-established bodies of theory and research in areas such as attitude formation and change, attribution, stereotyping and prejudice, and group dynamics. Nevertheless, there was a growing feeling that the discipline wasn't getting anywhere. Many questions that had originally prompted research programmes remained without clear answers, and some writers began to voice their concern that the wholesale adoption of the experimental method in social psychology had led to sophisticated technical advances not matched by advances in the understanding of social phenomena. Many felt that the artificial world of the laboratory could not simulate the complexity of human social experience. It was felt that important contextual features that give our behaviour its meaning were being systematically filtered out of experiments as contaminating variables and both the ethics of deception and the status of the relationship between experimenter and subject were brought into question (e.g. Armistead, 1974; Elms, 1975; see Parker, 1989, for a full analysis of the crisis).

Behaviourism had early given way to cognitive psychology as the dominant influence on social psychology, but the latter was no more social in its orientation, substituting information processing for the S–R bond* as its root explanation for human events. Some, like Gergen (1973), went further and suggested that human experience and social phenomena shift and change as cultural and societal circumstances change. The best we can hope for, he argued, is an historical analysis of the different questions

---

* According to learning theory, a stimulus (S) and a response (R) became associated or 'bonded' together through repeated reinforcement (reward).

social psychology has chosen to address at different times. In Europe, the hegemony of North American social psychology began to be challenged by writers such as Henri Tajfel and Serge Moscovici (drawing influence from Durkheim), who argued for a social psychology that recognises the social embeddedness of the individual. This concern is evident in their work, for example Tajfel's research on intergroup processes (see Chapter 4) and Moscovici's development of the theory of social representations (see Chapter 5), although, as Farr (1996) points out, Tajfel's social psychology was closer to the North American tradition in his use of laboratory experiments.

The dominant form of social psychology has therefore not been without its critics, and towards the end of the twentieth century social psychology has seen the emergence of strands of theory and research that radically depart from the individualism and experimentalism of earlier times. The emergence of critical social psychology (e.g. Stainton-Rogers *et al.*, 1995; Ibanez and Iniguez, 1997), social constructionism (see Burr, 1995; Parker, 1998a; Gergen, 1999) and discursive psychology (Edwards and Potter, 1992; Potter, 1996) represents a new move in psychology toward a social conception of the person. These theoretical approaches are accompanied by a preference for qualitative, non-experimental forms of enquiry. Ironically, however, there is little dialogue between the newer and older social psychologies, so that what we may be seeing here is the most recent incarnation of the long-standing division between psychological and sociological forms of the discipline.

Summary

The above account characterises social psychology as split along three dimensions: psychological vs. sociological in discipline location, individual vs. social in emphasis and North American vs. European in origin. However, although there is a good deal of overlap between them, it is not possible to simply map these dimensions on to each other. For example, we have seen that

21

European psychology contributed to the individualisation of social psychology through the use of experimentation and the subjective focus of Gestalt psychology, and symbolic interactionism, one of the most social of social psychologies originated in North America. Recent developments in critical social psychology and social constructionism, while having important roots in European philosophy, have included significant North American contributions. However, it is true to say that social psychology as a psychology of individuals has been heavily influenced by the history of psychology in North America and that the possibilities for a more *social* social psychology began a separate life under the auspices of sociology. Indeed, one could even say that the segregation of psychology and sociology as two separate disciplines was, at least in part, driven by the individualistic turn that social psychology took in North America. Farr (1996, p. 21) argues that 'If psychologists in America had accepted the social psychology of Mead then the gap between psychology and sociology would not have been so great as it is in the modern era.'

What, then is the model of the person implicit within the dominant form of social psychology familiar to psychologists today? Jackson (1988) argues that social psychology has never had a single and unified model of the person, and that its history could be seen as the search for one. Nevertheless, he claims that the experimental tradition has made implicit a model of the person as '*a passive, unreflexive, autonomous* individual whose behaviour is activated by aspects of the external world' (p. 108, italics in original). (This passivity and lack of reflexivity is certainly characteristic of the behaviourist tradition that was predominant for much of the first half of the twentieth century, although it may be less true of some of the more recent cognitive theories.) We can add to this that the individual pre-exists society, and can be understood independently of it. Social psychologists' interest has therefore been in how the social impacts upon this pre-existing individual. Indeed, the legacy of the Enlightenment period and of psychologists' early attempts to understand organised revolt and crowd behaviour has produced an entrenched assumption that the normal individual becomes abnormal when a member of a crowd or group, suffering loss of reason and intelligence and having a diminished sense of responsibility.

Overview of the rest of this book

In Chapter 2, I will begin to challenge the individualistic, pre-social conception of the person by taking a fresh look at some classic research in social psychology. By looking at work in the fields of attitudes, conformity, obedience and bystander apathy, I will argue that the findings of this research are better understood if we take a view of the person as more socially embedded.

I continue with the strategy of examining classic social psychological studies in Chapter 3, beginning with the infamous 'Stanford Prison Experiment', to show the importance of social roles in shaping our behaviour and experience. I then go on to consider the much broader appreciation of role-taking as it is understood in symbolic interactionism, and how this leads us to a notion of the person as socially negotiated and produced.

Chapter 4 continues with this theme, this time focusing upon the social psychology of groups. Beginning with an examination of the work on intergroup conflict, minimal groups and social identity theory, I show how social groups are important sources of personal identity. Through the concept of the 'reference group', I link this psychological social psychology with concepts from sociological social psychology, such as the generalised other, the looking-glass self, labelling and self-fulfilling prophecy, in order to further demonstrate the origins of the person in social relationships and social interaction.

In Chapter 5 the theme of the social origins of the person is considered with respect to theories that have concentrated on the role of culture and language. Social representations theory, discourse psychology and social constructionism are examined. Each of these in some way proposes that there is a socially produced and shared set of resources for making sense of the world and they emphasise the importance of language in producing, maintaining and changing these meanings.

Finally, Chapter 6 examines the nature of the person in social psychology through a discussion of three issues. Firstly, the different varieties of social psychology that have been discussed throughout the book are examined and I ask in what ways they can be considered *social* psychologies. The nature of the relationship between the individual and society is then considered, focusing upon the degree to which the person can be seen as preexisting society or as produced by it. Lastly, I consider the implications of these models for personal agency, choice and change.

Suggested further reading

Farr, R.M. (1996) *The roots of modern social psychology.* Oxford: Blackwell.

Graumann, C.F. (1988) 'Introduction to a history of social psychology', in M. Hewstone, W. Stroebe, J.P. Codol, and G.M. Stephenson (eds) *Introduction to social psychology.* Oxford: Blackwell.

Chapter 2

The social origins of behaviour

I N THE SUMMARY at the end of Chapter 1, I presented the person as represented within the kinds of social psychology that have dominated the field throughout most of the twentieth century. The behaviourist influence has rendered the person passive and unreflexive, his or her behaviour being in some way evoked by social situations without the mediation of thought. The experimental tradition gives us an individual that can be understood independently of society, even when we are attempting to explain the person's social behaviour. The 'ideology of the individual' that Farr (1996) talks about and that has been part of our common-sense understanding of what it means to be a person (in Western societies) defines this pre-social individual as normal. Against this normality, the changes that are observed in the person in group contexts come to be seen as abnormal and pathological, characterised by irrationality and irresponsibility. In the present chapter, my aim is to show how this vision of the person can be questioned by taking a fresh look at some of the classic research studies in social psychology – studies that have themselves helped to fashion the model of the person that I now want to challenge.

The situation specificity of behaviour

The first task is to question social psychology's focus upon the internal psychological properties and processes of individuals. The point I will make is that people's behaviour is very context-dependent. We tend to think of ourselves as pretty much the same kind of person from day to day and from place to place, and this view of ourselves as consistent and coherent individuals can be thought of as part of the ideology mentioned above; it is often more a description of what we feel *ought* to be the case than of what actually happens (Gergen, 1972). The term 'situation specificity' is usually associated with early versions of social learning theory (e.g. Mischel, 1968), and refers to the claim that our behaviour is dependent upon the situation or context in which we find ourselves, rather than the outcome of internal processes. The claim that behaviour is situation specific challenges the essentialist assumptions of trait and type theories of personality. For example, honesty had long been found to refer not so much to a reliable and consistent aspect of the personality than to aspects of behaviour in certain circumstances (Hartshorne and May, 1928–1930). But in social psychology the relevance of situation specificity is seen most clearly in the study of attitudes.

A central question for social psychologists has been the nature of the relationship between attitudes and behaviour. Paradoxically, the term 'attitude', when it was first used by social scientists, referred to *social* attitudes. W.I. Thomas, a sociologist at Chicago University at the time of Mead, saw the study of attitudes as the most important task of social psychology and it has occupied a central place in the discipline throughout most of its history. Thomas was also a student of Wundt and inherited his interest in shared cultural beliefs and practices. For Thomas, social attitudes were the subjective components of culture and constituted important characteristic features of communities. But the term 'attitude' today has a more individualistic feel; we think of an attitude as something private and internal to a person, something characteristic of the way a person thinks, and this is the meaning of 'attitude' in contemporary research. To what extent, then, is our behaviour the outcome of the attitudes we hold?

There has been a considerable tendency, in the body of theory relating to attitudes, to assume that attitudes and behaviour are related, and that attitudes at least partly determine our behaviour (e.g. Ajzen and Fishbein, 1977). However, Wicker (1969), after reviewing a great deal of the empirical research on the attitude–behaviour link, concluded that the relationship between overt behaviour and measured attitudes may be very weak. One of the earliest and best-known studies is that of La Pière (1934). La Pière was a sociologist, so it is interesting to note that this study was not a laboratory experiment, as would have been favoured by psychologists of his day. La Pière took advantage of a situation that found him travelling around the United States in the company of a Chinese couple. Given the prejudice against the Chinese in the USA at the time, La Pière fully expected to have some difficulty when it came to their reception in hotels and restaurants. During their travels, they visited 251 establishments and, to La Pière's surprise, were refused service at only one. Six months later, La Pière wrote to each of the establishments they had visited asking if they would accept Chinese people as guests. Only 128 replies were received, but of those 92% said that they would not accept Chinese people as guests. A similar refusal rate was found in a control sample of similar establishments that had not been visited. Clearly, in the case of large numbers of the proprietors of the hotels and restaurants visited by La Pière and the Chinese couple, stated attitudes were not a reliable indication of overt behaviour.

Numerous explanations have been put forward for these findings. It has been suggested that the proprietors' response may have been influenced by the fact that the Chinese couple was well dressed and spoke good English. They may have been motivated more by their reluctance to turn away business than by their prejudice, or they may have feared the consequences of making a scene in front of other guests. Turning away guests may also have conflicted with their role as a welcoming host. All these points are good ones, and these kinds of considerations have led to the preference of contemporary attitude researchers for being very specific about the conditions under which we can expect to find a relationship between behaviour and stated attitude, for example Fishbein and Ajzen's (1975) theory of reasoned action. But my point is that, rather than see the social realm as a set of variables that can be shown to have some (albeit complex) effect upon intra-psychic processes, we might understand human conduct better if we see the social context as the place where our action derives its meaning – literally 'where the action is'! This does not mean that we should ignore intra-psychic processes or consider them irrelevant – but it means that our investigations should focus much more on the nature of the social context than has previously been the case.

Further doubt about the role of attitudes in producing behaviour comes from Festinger's (1957) theory of cognitive dissonance. Festinger and his associates conducted a series of experiments in which participants were induced to perform behaviours towards which they were likely to hold negative attitudes. Typically, participants were given a very boring task to perform, under the impression that this was the experiment they had been asked to take part in. They were then asked to explain to another potential subject just how interesting and exciting they had found the experimental task. They found that, in the absence of any other justification (such as a sizeable payment for complying with this request) participants would afterwards express positive attitudes towards the task in order to rationalise their behaviour. Festinger was interested in the implications that this research had for the notion of cognitive consistency. This is the idea that we like our thoughts, feelings and behaviours to be consistent with each other, and when we find ourselves in a situation where they are inconsistent or dissonant we feel uncomfortable. Under these conditions we do whatever we can to bring everything back into line, such as changing our attitude. But we can draw two further implications from these studies.

Firstly, they put a fresh complexion on the relationship between attitudes and behaviour; it appears that our behaviour is just as likely to produce our attitudes as the reverse. But they also signal that our behaviour just isn't planned or caused in any simple way. The participants in Festinger's studies found themselves acting in a way that they later needed to justify. The request put to the participants (to say positive things about the task to a waiting subject in the next room) was very carefully stage-managed to appear outside of the experiment. The experimenter sheepishly related how they had been let down by the person who usually performed this part of the experiment, that, once the participants had gained some experience at the job, they might be called on again in the future (and expect similar payment), and that it would only take a few minutes of their time (Festinger and Carlsmith, 1959). The participants therefore found themselves in a familiar social interaction: that of being asked to do something as a favour for someone. There can be few of us who haven't at some time uttered the words 'I don't know why I agreed to do it' or 'I should never have let myself get talked into it', and these reflections testify to the way in which our behaviour arises spontaneously out of social situations. We can look back and think of all sorts of reasons why we shouldn't (or should!) have done something, but at the time we were carried along on a tide of social interaction, caught up in a complex social system involving what it means to us to receive and respond to a request for help. This is a meaning that is of course fundamentally a culturally shared one.

Theories like those of Fishbein and Ajzen (1975) and Festinger (1957) firmly locate attitudes as psychological rather than social phenomena, and our attention thus becomes drawn away from the social context that gives our behaviour its meaning. The notion of attitudes as private mental properties that influence our behaviour appears to have very limited usefulness in our attempts to understanding human conduct, whereas the social situation forming the context for the behaviour gives our conduct its rationale. It could thus be argued that our current efforts to retain the concept of attitude, as an individual mental property, explain more about the long-standing investment in our implicit model of the individual person than about the origins of our conduct; to reverse the usual homily, if we didn't already have our current concept of 'attitude', it would *not* be necessary to invent it! Further research evidence from the field of attitudes and prejudice supports the view that we cannot understand people's behaviour by appealing to intra-psychic (that is, purely contained within an individual's mind) structures but must look outward to the social context for our understanding. Minard (1952) studied a mining community in Virginia, USA. The community consisted of both black and white people, and below ground both blacks and whites worked together without difficulty. However, the prejudice and segregation that was part of the cultural life of the mining town came to the fore at the end of the working day. Brown (1995) illustrates this with a quote from one of Minard's interviewees:

> Do you see that bus there? [pointing to the miner's bus which took them to and from the pit]. The men ride in that bus all mixed up together and pay no attention. A white man sits with a Negro or anyway just however it comes handy. Nobody cares or pays any attention. But the white man will get right off that bus and on the interstate bus and he will not sit near a Negro.
>
> (Minard, 1952, p. 31)

This suggests that the social norms operating above and below ground were more important than intra-psychic factors such as attitudes in producing the workers' behaviour towards each other.

The concept of norms is one I will return to later in this chapter. But for the moment my reason for discussing this attitude research is to illustrate some points about the nature of the person in social psychology. The first is that we cannot adequately understand people's social behaviour by an appeal to what we believe are stable characteristics of their psychology, such as personality or attitudes. Also, how people behave varies too much from situation to situation for this to be feasible. The workers in Minard's study were the same people above and below ground, but their behaviour was different. The individual may therefore be a less consistent and coherent being than has been assumed by psychology and social psychology. But although our behaviour changes with the social context these changes are not arbitrary or random; our behaviour makes sense when we locate it within the patterns of assumptions, traditions and ways of life of the social group we are acting within. We may not feel that we can defend some of the conduct of the townspeople in Minard's study, but we do understand it. We wonder at the behaviour of Festinger and Carlsmith's participants until we see them as responding in an appropriate manner to a request for assistance during a familiar social interaction. A proper understanding of the person therefore requires that we locate them in their social context. This does not mean that we have to have intimate knowledge of a person's life history and cultural origins before we can understand their conduct (although it might). But at the very least it means we have to know something of the immediate social context of a person's behaviour in order to appreciate its meaning and rationale. Behaviour, like quotations, can be misleading when taken out of context.

Situational demands

The fact that the situations people find themselves in can exert a strong pull on their behaviour has not gone unnoticed by psychologists. Interestingly, it was in the context of laboratory experiments that these demand characteristics have particularly been studied. A key figure in the study of demand characteristics is Martin Orne. Orne was working in the field of hypnosis, and was interested in devising ways of finding out whether hypnotised people were able to do or were prepared to do things that non-hypnotised people did not. In fact he found it was extraordinarily difficult to come up with anything that could distinguish between hypnotised people and those who had just been asked to act as if they were hypnotised. For example, participants in his experiments were prepared to persevere at boring and fruitless tasks for long periods of time. It seemed that, having agreed to take part in a psychology experiment, the participants had implicitly committed themselves to doing whatever the experimenter asked of them, no matter how unreasonable their request might otherwise have appeared.

Orne (1962) suggested that this implicit commitment to carry out the experimenter's requests was part of a general motivation to be a good subject. Orne's participants were doing whatever was necessary to comply with what the situation demanded, to properly perform their role as a subject in a psychology experiment. Furthermore, Orne's studies suggested that not only did their commitment involve conscientiously carrying out the experimenter's requests, but participants showed that they were interested in what the experiment was about. They formed an impression of what the researcher expected the experiment to prove (the hypothesis) and did their best to help. The potential for participants' own ideas about the experimental hypothesis to affect the results was found to be considerable, and it became necessary to recommend the use of rigorous research designs (for example double-blind conditions) to offset these effects. The term 'demand characteristics' is therefore perhaps rather misleading. It has a behaviouristic flavour that is inappropriate here. Orne's participants were not passively responding to certain features of the experimental situation: they were curious about it and actively engaged in building up their own theories of what the experimenter might be trying to prove.

The study of demand characteristics therefore provides us with two more important considerations regarding the person. The first is that, although social psychology experiments are designed and reported as if their participants were simply responding to the stimulus conditions set up by the experimenter, in fact they are doing what they would do in any other social situation: trying to understand it and take part in it in a meaningful way. Participants in social psychology experiments are therefore by no means passive recipients of stimuli. Secondly, it requires us to think of the social psychology experiment as, in essential respects, the same as other social situations in which a person finds himself or herself. Of course, the rules for appropriate behaviour in these situations may be somewhat unusual or difficult to fathom. So the experiment is a rather bizarre kind of social interaction. But, as in other forms of social interaction, the person's task is to act appropriately. Looked at in this way, psychology experiments can never isolate their participants from the contamination of social variables, since the experiment itself *is* a social situation:

> Imagine that you are asked to act as a subject in a laboratory experiment. The first thing you are likely to do is start wondering about what the experimenter is 'really' up to. When you enter the laboratory, you do not enter a cultural vacuum. On the contrary, you enter the laboratory with a host of ideas and expectations about what a laboratory experiment is, and about the role and character of psychologists and psychological research, among other things. . . . An essential part of the culture in the laboratory context are the roles of the subject and the experimenter. These roles are based on a number of shared understandings about the nature of science and of research, and about what researchers and human subjects are supposed to do.
>
> (Moghaddam *et al.*, 1993, p. 31)

It seems that, no matter what precautions are taken, people persist in behaving with reference to other persons in their social environment. The experimental tradition in psychology and social psychology has been based upon the implicit (or explicit) assumption that the individual in its pure state can be studied in the laboratory but even here we find it necessary to understand the person's behaviour as socially occasioned and socially meaningful. Having reached this point, we can begin to see the possibility for a rather different understanding of the individual. If we must repeatedly look to the social realm, to culture, social expectations and social interaction in order to understand a person's conduct, then perhaps this realm is primary. Rather than see the social realm as a source of influences that impact upon and moderate the behaviour of a pre-existing individual, we might see it as playing a much more important role in producing the features that we associate with being a person. It is important to be clear that this conceptualisation involves more than simply the argument that social situations can have a dramatic *impact* upon the individual (which is what social psychology itself has been saying all along). It is quite a different matter to suggest that we can't understand what it means to be a person without an understanding of the way in which the person is socially embedded. This is a theme that I will continue to explore throughout this book.

The assumption that social factors have an (albeit dramatic) impact upon the pre-existing individual is axiomatic to what has in the past been a central research area for social psychology: that of social influence. This covers a broad spectrum of related phenomena such as conformity, compliance and obedience. It is therefore appropriate to now take a fresh look at this field to continue our re-examination of the person in social psychology.

Social influence

Social norms

A good deal of social psychological research in the mid-twentieth century was devoted to the question of social influence. The atrocities of the Second World War were still fresh in people's minds. It was evident that ordinary people could, under certain conditions, do terrible things; you don't have to be a psychopath to kill someone, you just need to be following orders or doing what everyone else does. Much of the research on social influence has focused on the effects of group membership and peer pressure on the behaviour and judgements of individuals, and in particular on the effects of the judgements of a consistent majority on those of single individuals. This research focus in itself demonstrates the conception of the individual in modern Western society. There is considerable concern here that rational, moral and free-thinking individuals may be unduly influenced by their peer group if they find that their own personal views are unpopular or just uncommon. Interestingly, 'unpopular' means only that something lies outside of the rest of the population, that it is unusual. But the term has come to take on a value connotation, so that 'unpopular' means generally disliked. Thus the unusual is also often de-valued.

One of the earliest experiments on social influence was that of Muzafer Sherif (1935). He used the autokinetic effect to examine what happens when people make judgements of ambiguous stimuli. The autokinetic effect is a visual illusion. It is the apparent movement that we see when we observe a single point of light in a dark room. Sherif asked people to judge the amount of movement of the light (he did not tell them that the movement was illusory) over several trials. He found that, when they were asked to do this in groups with each person calling out their own judgement alongside their peers, the judgements quickly moved to a central norm. When they were subsequently asked to make judgements alone, their judgements retained the influence of the group norm. This result is perhaps unsurprising. When faced with an ambiguous stimulus, it is logical and perhaps necessary that we look to others for their opinion and use this as a guide in our own judgements. Nearly thirty years after Sherif's first experiment, Hood and Sherif (1962), again using the autokinetic effect, found similar influence of others' judgements on those of a single individual even when the subject only accidentally overheard those judgements. They conclude that the effect cannot therefore be considered social pressure (or 'normative influence'). Some writers have suggested that conformity may be a misleading description of what is happening in some situations where individuals appear to modify their behaviour in the direction of other group members. Particularly when we are unsure of the accuracy or legitimacy of our own view, we naturally and sensibly look to others for information. We know from experience that sometimes others have a more reliable or well-informed view and trusting the judgement of others is therefore something that we are all likely to find helpful from time to time. The term 'informational influence' has been used to describe occasions when we trust others' judgement more than our own. Again, there is nothing pathological or irrational about this; it may in fact be highly adaptive. Without our ability to draw on others' knowledge and experience we would have only our own, necessarily more limited, repertoire to inform our decisions.

But there is something more to be said about what is happening here. People were not just using others' judgements in a haphazard way. Their judgements were coordinated in such a way that, without their realising it, between them they negotiated a group norm. This cannot be conceptualised as a one-way influence of any one person or many people upon another individual's judgement. The construction of this group norm was a joint project in which all played a part and yet in which the particular part played by each was impossible to isolate. The notion of a group norm is therefore an explanatory concept of the same kind suggested by Le Bon and others in the early days of social psychology. It is a concept that works not at the level of the individual but at the level of the collectivity.

The ideology of the individual puts conformity to social norms in a poor light. The rational and free-thinking individual of the Enlightenment doesn't simply accept the forms of thought and behaviour of peers but makes up his or her own mind about things. The people of the twentieth century have perhaps been the most vociferous in exhorting us not to be constrained by convention, to pursue our goals and speak our minds even if it does mean ruffling the feathers of those who are more worried about what the neighbours might think than about truth or happiness. But in our rush to extol the virtues of independent thought and action we should not lose sight of the crucial role that social norms play in our lives. It would be a disaster if we all independently decided which side of the road to drive on or decided to develop and speak only our own personal language. There could be no society without some conventions; they may be arbitrary but as long as everyone agrees to conform to them we can have some meaningful dealings with each other. Norms surrounding what, when and how to eat, what kind of houses to live in or how to spend our leisure time are not simply unthinking habits that we have copied from others. They are the frameworks around which we can build kinship and friendship networks. And when we find ourselves in a situation we have never met with before, when we simply don't know how to act, social norms can provide an answer. Societies would not be possible without social norms, and we may regard the ease with which human beings can develop such norms between themselves as one reason for why we have societies at all, and for their longevity and diversity.

Conformity under peer pressure

However, the emergence of social norms was not the aspect of Sherif's findings that captured the imagination of social psychologists at the time. The issue was rather framed in terms of conformity. It appeared that participants might be conforming rather than acting independently, and there was a concern to discover whether the influence of others' judgements really changed an individual's own perception or simply led to compliance. The stimulus used by Sherif was intentionally ambiguous, and so was not considered a rigorous enough test of the extent to which people are prepared to conform or comply with others' views. What would people do if they were faced with a situation where they could be certain of their own perception and yet find themselves in disagreement with their peers? Would they behave independently and refuse to be swayed from their own judgement? Would they comply and go along with the others, but privately hold on to their own view? Or would their perception be distorted by others' judgements, so that they end up conforming because they have internalised others' judgements?

The famous series of experiments carried out by Solomon Asch in the 1950s (e.g. Asch, 1956) was intended to answer these questions. Asch used North American college students and typically placed one naïve subject in a group of confederates and presented the group with a simple task. They were to judge the lengths of a number of straight lines by comparing them to a standard stimulus line. In each trial, the task was to select from an array of lines the one that was nearest to the standard in length, and the participants were required to each give their judgements in turn, with the naïve subject typically in the second-to-last position. On approximately two-thirds of the trials, all the confederates of the experimenter were instructed to give the same wrong answer. Asch found that naïve participants made the same judgement as the confederates on approximately 37% of these trials. Individual participants varied in the numbers of erroneous judgements they gave, with some conforming on several trials and some only occasionally. But only about 25% of them didn't conform at all.

These findings seem to legitimate the suspicion that the judgement and reasoning of individuals becomes weakened in a group situation. Unlike Sherif's experiment, the task here did not involve an ambiguous stimulus. Asch's participants appear to deny the evidence of their own eyes in order to conform to the judgements of the majority. They were not coerced or even encouraged, there were no material consequences dependent upon their judgement, and they owed no particular allegiance to the others in their group; in fact they were strangers. However, it was clear from the video recordings of the experiments that the naïve participants were suffering a good deal of discomfort and anxiety. When they were interviewed afterwards, the participants who had conformed talked about what had happened. Some of them reported that they did actually see the lines in the way that the confederates did; in other words, their perception was actually altered. Others had not in fact agreed with the majority view, but said they had just gone along with it because they didn't want to feel different from the others.

Numerous experiments followed those of Asch, and replication studies continued to be performed throughout the 1970s and 1980s, on North American samples and also using people from other countries. Levels of conformity, not surprisingly, have been found to vary according to particular features of the experimental design and across cultures, and it is possible to point to a wide variety of factors that contribute to the production of conformity in these studies. There has been some suggestion that the levels of conformity found in Asch's studies should be seen as a product of the North American 'zeitgeist' (spirit of the times) in the 1950s. This was the McCarthy era, when it was import-ant to show solidarity with your peers as a good American against what was seen as the threat of communism. Some later studies in the 1970s and 1980s did indeed find lower levels of confor-mity, suggesting that changes in the cultural climate away from conformity and towards an emphasis on independence of thought could be responsible. For example, Larsen (1974) found much less conformity in a sample of North American students, Perrin and Spencer (1981) found almost no conformity in their British study, and Nicholson et al. (1985) found very low levels of confor-mity in both North American and British students. However, it has been pointed out that Perrin and Spencer's participants were students of engineering, mathematics and chemistry and that they would be just the kind of people who would have a high invest-ment in their own accuracy of judgement (Brown, 1996).

In addition, although some studies did find reduced levels of conformity, others have found similar levels in participants from many different countries. According to van Avermaet (1988) studies in the Netherlands and Belgium have found similar results to those of Asch; and Moghaddam et al. (1993) report a num-ber of studies finding similar or greater levels of conformity in people from Brazil, China, Fiji and Rhodesia (now Zimbabwe). But Moghaddam et al. also report studies finding less con-formity among German and Japanese participants, and they argue that differences in levels of conformity are related to specific cultural val-ues for conformity or independence. They argue that German and Japanese cultures are characterised by strong loyalties to particular, well-defined groups and by conformity to these groups but not to groups of strangers in a laboratory experiment. They also cite evi-dence suggesting that the value placed upon bringing up children to be self-reliant and independent is characteristic of industrialised countries like the USA, whereas countries such as Indonesia and Turkey emphasise the need for children to be brought up to obey their parents. Moghaddam *et al.* suggest that it is the greater social and geographical mobility in the populations of industrialised countries that contributes to this emphasis upon independence and self-reliance. Family, community and tribal ties become weakened and thus less influential in such circumstances. Therefore the propensity for people to submit to peer pressure in experiments of the kind devised by Asch may depend upon subtle variations in culturally shared values for independence and self-reliance, solidarity, group identity and compliance with others' wishes.

It is usually assumed that it is peer pressure that is operating in such experiments, given the comments made by some of Asch's participants who didn't want to be seen as different from the others. However, over and above the cultural factors just discussed, there may be further reasons to believe that conformity effects are not so straightforward. Perrin and Spencer's (1981) study included variations in which the experimenter, confederates and naïve participants were differentially drawn from a non-student sample that included whites and West Indians, probationers and probation officers. They found levels of compliance similar to those found by Asch when the experimenter was white and the naïve subject was West Indian, and when the experimenter and confederates were probation officers and the naïve subject was on probation. Perrin and Spencer concluded that people conform when they feel that the personal costs of not doing so are too great. Asch's studies were not exempt from such considerations. Although both confederates and students were drawn from a student population the experimenter was a university lecturer and the students were taking part in the experiment as part of their course requirements. The situation was therefore quite complicated in terms of the field of expectations, duties, status and power inequalities present. One might reasonably expect that participants in these experiments are struggling with a number of implicit questions: What is the experimenter trying to prove? How can I be a good subject? How am I supposed to behave? Will I spoil the experiment if I agree/disagree with the others? What will the experimenter think of me if I agree/disagree? What will the others think? Will their opinions have consequences for me? Although the stimulus material used in these experiments was not in itself ambiguous, nevertheless it could be said that the situation in which participants found themselves was indeed ambiguous. Adherence to the group norm can therefore be seen as a parsimonious solution. In addition, the subject knows that the tasks used in laboratory experiments do not have consequences in the real world; the judgement the subject makes only has implications for their role as subject and for any social relationship they may have with the experimenter and other participants outside of the laboratory. It therefore does not seem irrational or irresponsible for their decisions to be based upon these considerations. Just how each of the participants weighed up these considerations may help us to understand the individual differences in conformity levels. Asch demonstrated that the conformity effect was drastically reduced when an ally was placed among the confederates, providing moral support and reassurance that, whatever the outcome, the subject will not be alone in bearing the consequences.

It has sometimes been pointed out that in all of the conformity studies that have been carried out participants actually did not conform with their peers on the majority of trials (about 63%). One could regard this as evidence that it is normally rather difficult to get people to conform to a majority view that differs from their own and that it is our entrenched fear of social influence that sensitises us to it when it does occur. I mentioned at the beginning of this section that most work on conformity has concentrated on the effects of the majority upon the individual, and that this in itself illustrates our preoccupation with preserving what we see as the integrity of the self-contained individual. However, this is not the only question that can be asked about social influence, as Moscovici et al. (1969, pp. 531–532) point out:

> . . . when examining the individual, it is always assumed that
> he [sic] asks himself the question 'should I follow the group
> or the minority?' or in other words he is faced with the
> alternative of conformity or deviance. On the contrary, an

individual frequently poses the question in exactly the inverse manner: 'What should I do so that the majority will adopt my point of view? How can I change the conception of others?'

Moscovici has been critical of social psychology's preoccupation with individual functioning at the expense of an understanding of social context and history. In the field of social influence, Moscovici's major contribution was a series of experiments that turned the traditional paradigm upside-down and asked what effect a single person can have upon the view of a majority. Indeed, without the possibility that minorities and individuals could sway majority opinion it is difficult to see how important new ideas or social change could come about. Although his use of laboratory experiments does not differentiate him from North American social psychologists, his research paradigm made it possible to consider the importance of the *pattern* of a person's judgements over time. Moscovici demonstrated that a lone voice could be influential, if the person was consistent in their judgement over time, and could lead to a previously unconvinced majority adopting the minority position. This suggests that, when we are weighing up the legitimacy of someone's view, we do so in a temporal context. We take into consideration what the person has said on previous occasions. This has similarities to Kelley's (1967) covariation model of attribution (see Chapter 6). Kelley's model is thought to have an advantage over other models of attribution because it allows for the way in which people naturally take into account how someone has behaved on past, similar occasions and across a variety of situations when making a judgement about them. Like Kelley, Moscovici therefore alerts us to the fact that in real life our judgements are never made in a historical vacuum. Incidentally, his work also demonstrates that individuals are quite capable of resisting social pressures to conform to the majority view.

Ultimately, the conformity vs. independence dichotomy may be ill-conceived. If we reflect upon examples of what we mean by conformity and independence we can see that they are not so easily distinguishable. Is the Teddy Boy, the Rocker, the Punk or Skinhead an independent thinker, challenging conventional codes of behaviour and dress? Or a conformist to the norms of their own sub-culture? Should we call someone independent who steadfastly refuses to change their opinion despite overwhelming evidence that they are wrong? Are those who repeatedly flout or ignore accepted codes of conduct, rules and laws non-conformists, mentally ill or criminals? Answers to such questions are not easy, and demonstrate that the value we apparently place on the independent thinker depends upon first ruling out a great number of people and behaviours that we would logically need to include. And being independent of one set of norms or values can very often be seen as just conformity to a different set. In this sense, I think it is possible to say that we are *always* behaving with regard to others in some way. Even the person who remains steadfast in the face of persuasion or coercion is behaving in relation to those persuading or coercing others; their independence is in fact defined by those others. For the person who strives, in bringing up their children, to reject the methods of their own parents it is ironically the latter who are most present, most relevant to their own behaviour. Whether we adopt or reject the views and ways of others our own choices are therefore always made with reference *to* them. However we act, our conduct is always and necessarily defined in terms of shared social meanings.

Obedience

Stanley Milgram's experimental studies of obedience at Yale University in the early 1960s (later brought together and reported in his 1974 book *Obedience to authority*) are perhaps the best-known in social psychology. The research was explicitly a response to the routine slaughter of the Jews during the Second World War, and Milgram (1963) points out quite simply that: 'These inhumane policies may have originated in the mind of a single person, but they could only be carried out on a massive scale if a very large number of persons obeyed orders' (p. 93). He then goes on to suggest that: 'Facts of recent history and observation in daily life suggest that for many persons obedience may be a deeply ingrained behavior tendency, indeed, a prepotent impulse overriding training in ethics, sympathy and moral conduct' (p. 93). Some historians had proposed the idea that the mass destruction of the Jews in Nazi Germany was only possible because of a basic flaw in the German national character, a predisposition to blind obedience. Milgram's original plan was to study levels of obedience in both North American and German populations, and he was expecting little routine obedience from the former.

Milgram's experimental paradigm is now generally well known: naïve participants are deceived by the experimenter and believe they are taking part in an experiment to establish the effects of punishment on learning. The participants, who were paid volunteers from all walks of life, were required to deliver what they believed to be increasingly painful electric shocks to a learner (who was in fact a confederate of the experimenter) each time the learner made an error on a learning task (no shock was in fact delivered). Milgram's measure of obedience was the level of shock that the subject was prepared to administer before refusing to continue. If participants showed unwillingness to carry on at any point, they were encouraged by emphatic prompts from the experimenter to continue. The experiment included increasingly distressing protests from the learner as the 'shocks' became more painful. Prior to carrying out the experiments, Milgram asked a sample of psychology students at Yale University to estimate the percentage of people who they thought would continue with the procedure up to the highest level of shock, and none predicted more than 3%. In the event, Milgram found that substantial proportions of participants were prepared to deliver shocks of up to 450 volts. For example, Milgram (1963) found that 26 out of 40 (65%) participants did so, with no subject stopping before 300 volts.

It appeared that a predisposition to obedience was not a personality disorder characteristic of certain people or nations, and Milgram, surprised and saddened by his findings, never carried out a comparative study in Germany. His studies created a great deal of controversy, and this was partly because they had unwelcome implications:

> The results were unpalatable because they demonstrated that it is the situations in which people find themselves (and that such situations can be very easily arranged) rather than their predispositions or character traits which lead them to act the way they do. In societies where emphasis is placed on people's responsibility for their own actions and where many psychological theories emphasise 'agency' and people's ability to initiate actions and control events, . . . such findings are more disturbing than the thought that evil deeds are done by a few pathological people.
>
> (Brown, 1996, p. 23)

Commenting upon our surprise and concern at the readiness with which ordinary citizens obeyed the experimenter's instructions, Moghaddam *et al.* (1993) argue that, since in many cultures individualism and individual freedom are less prominent, the findings of social influence studies is seen as unsurprising in these cultures. For example, in Japan the emphasis is on a person's obligations to society rather than their personal freedom. Japanese people would be surprised if individuals were found *not* to be influenced by others.

There are a number of factors that could be contributing to Milgram's findings. The participants were paid volunteers, and were probably highly motivated to perform their role properly and fully: to be good participants. They were taking part in an experiment in a prestigious university, whose staff had unquestionable reputations. In later experiments, Milgram found that reducing the apparent status of the location and/or the experimenter significantly reduced obedience. The participants believed that all the participants in the experiment were there voluntarily and not in any way coerced, including the learner. They were reassured by the experimenter that the shocks would be 'painful but not dangerous', and may at some level have retained the belief that no harm would be done. In fact, Orne and Evans (1965) demonstrated that participants are prepared to carry out what appeared to be dangerous acts because of their ultimate belief that the experimenter would not ask them to do anything that could really be harmful. In sum, the subject is here placed in an unusual and complex situation where tried and tested rules of thumb for our everyday moral behaviour may seem of little utility.

The impact of Milgram's research was in its shocking implication that ordinary people, who were not coerced or threatened and who could not be said to suffer from any pathological personality condition, could cause harm to another person simply because they were told to do so by someone in a position of authority. This appears a strong signal of the extent to which the morality and responsibility of the individual can be quickly undermined by social influence. Many reports of Milgram's research in social psychology text books seem prepared to leave it at that. But Milgram himself had interesting theoretical points to make that locate his findings in a wider social and evolutionary context. He argued that people living in organised, hierarchical societies move between two different states governing their behaviour: the autonomous state and the agentic state. In the autonomous state, our actions are voluntary and subject to the dictates of conscience. In the agentic state, we see ourselves as the agents of others, performing behaviours on their behalf, and individual conscience is not active. In the agentic state, people no longer feel responsible for their actions, but instead feel responsible to the person in authority and are concerned to carry out their duties properly. The agentic state, and the obedience it requires, is in itself vital to the operation of organised societies. Philip Meyer, in a 1972 magazine article provocatively entitled 'If Hitler asked you to electrocute a stranger, would you? Probably', says this:

> Without obedience to a relevant ruling authority, there could
> not be a civil society. . . . Would we really want a situation
> in which every participant in a war, direct or indirect – from
> front-line soldiers to the people who sell coffee and ciga-
> rettes to employees at the Concertina barbed-wire factory in
> Kansas – stops and consults his conscience before each
> action. . . . When Francis Gary Powers was being tried by

a Soviet military tribunal after his U-2 spy plane was shot down, the presiding judge asked if he had thought about the possibility that his flight might have provoked a war. Powers replied with Hobbesian clarity: 'The people who sent me should think of these things. My job was to carry out orders. I do not think it was my responsibility to make such decisions.'

It was not his responsibility. And it is quite possible that if everyone felt responsible for each of the ultimate consequences of his own tiny contributions to complex chains of events, then society simply would not work.

(pp. 143–144)

In a hierarchical society or organisation, we each sacrifice some control over our own actions and accept some control from a superior in the hierarchy, and it may be argued that, regardless of its shortcomings, this coordinated, hierarchically arranged activity is necessary for the creation of products that potentially benefit the whole society rather than single individuals. For Milgram, the dilemma faced by his participants was brought about by a conflict between the autonomous and agentic modes of behaviour. His participants demonstrated sometimes extreme levels of tension and anxiety before they finally decided to disobey the experimenter's instructions, a testimony to the conflict they were experiencing: '. . . the conflict stems from the opposition of two deeply ingrained behavior dispositions: first, the disposition not to harm other people, and second, the tendency to obey those whom we perceive to be legitimate authorities' (Milgram, 1963, p. 100). Thus, Milgram theoretically locates his findings within a wider phenomenon that he sees as broadly functional and necessary for societies.

A study by Hofling *et al.* (1966) (cited in Hayes, 1994) provides a useful illustration of obedience in a non-laboratory situation. This was a study of nurses' obedience to doctors in a hospital, and involved bogus phone calls to staff nurses on night duty. The calls were from a person who claimed to be a doctor and instructed the nurse to administer a drug to one of his patients. Despite the fact that hospital regulations forbade nurses to administer medication on the strength of telephone instructions, and despite the nurses being aware that the amount of medication instructed was in excess of that recommended on the drug label, most of the nurses in the experiment were prepared to obey the instructions (they were in fact prevented from actually carrying them out). When they were later interviewed, the nurses explained that doctors often gave instructions by telephone and became annoyed if nurses tried to follow hospital regulations by refusing to carry them out. The power imbalance between doctors and nurses made the latter sensitive to the possibility that annoying the doctors could affect their careers. Hospitals are hierarchical organisations, and it may be argued, in line with Milgram's theory, that this is why they are able to function reasonably efficiently and provide adequate care for large numbers of patients. If staff in positions lower down the hierarchy were not the obedient agents of those higher up, the system would fall apart. Given the way that hierarchies work, one can easily imagine situations arising where a subordinate, doubting the advisability of a superior's decision, acts autonomously with disastrous results. It is in the nature of hierarchies that those further up can see the bigger picture. This is not to say that they are always right, but the system can only work if each person delegates upwards some responsibility for decisions. The nurses' dilemma and ultimate decision to obey in Hofling's study seems reasonable in this light.

Diffusion of responsibility

The reduction in subjective responsibility and culpability suggested by studies of obedience is a concern that has also been raised by the famous 'bystander intervention' studies of Latané and Darley, also in the 1960s. The issue here was how an individual's sense of personal responsibility could become diluted in a group context. Research into bystander intervention was triggered by an account in the *New York Times* in March 1964 of what was seen at the time as an horrific crime. The facts that psychology students usually learn about this crime are that a young woman, Kitty

Genovese, was murdered on the street by a man unknown to her. He followed her as she walked home in the early hours one morning, then stabbed her numerous times. He raped her as she lay dying, a fact which sometimes is left out of accounts in psychology text books. Although 38 people heard her cries or witnessed some part of the events, no-one came to her aid or even called the police.

It was the inaction of these bystanders that was of interest and concern to the public, and to social psychologists. According to Cherry (1995), following the incident articles and letters were published in the *New York Times*, commenting upon and offering explanations for the crime. It was variously suggested that city life had become alienating and remote from human concerns, that the relatively well-heeled people of New York were no longer concerned about what happened on the streets outside of their own comfortable lives, or that the murder witnesses were grati-fying their own sadistic impulses. But as Latané and Darley (1968) point out, none of the many people writing these articles and letters felt that they themselves were alienated, indifferent or sadistic and the researchers doubted that the events could be explained in terms that left the majority of ordinary people squeaky-clean. They thought it likely that most people, if put in the same situation as those witnesses, would have found them-selves doing exactly the same. As social psychologists in the dominant tradition, they were interested in locating the situational variables that produce this bystander apathy.

Latané and Darley and their co-workers conducted a series of experiments in which some crisis would typically be enacted, perhaps an epileptic fit, smoke suggesting a fire in an adjacent room or the sound of someone falling and calling out nearby. The participants were college students who had been asked to take part in a study and were placed either alone or in groups in a waiting room. The results showed that people were more likely to notice the crisis and to respond to it when they were alone than when they were in groups. This is to some extent a counter-intuitive finding, since one might expect that the more people who see someone in a crisis the more likely it is that someone will come to their aid. Latané and Darley (1968) conclude that, when people are in the presence of others, they are less likely to notice an emergency, less likely to *define* the situation as an emergency, and less likely to take action. Not noticing and not defining the situation as an emergency both go some way toward explaining these findings, but Latané and Darley also suggest that individuals in groups experience a 'diffusion of responsibility'. When a person recognises that an emergency is taking place, they may still not take action because their sense of responsibility is diffused or diluted, like the soldier in the firing squad who does not feel personally responsible for the death of the victim. We do not take action because we feel that everyone else who is present is equally responsible. But the participants in these experiments could not be described as apathetic or indifferent: they were clearly distressed by the event and confused about what they should do. Latané and Darley conclude that it is not indifference that leads to inaction but the definition of the situation and diffused responsibility created by groups.

This research seems to confirm the fear that the moral sensibility of the individual is undermined in the group context. In this sense it is an illustrative example of the ideology of the individual who pre-exists society and is diluted by it. However, the definition of the situation is not a simple individual affair. Latané and Darley do not seem to be saying that individuals were influenced by definitions of the situation that had previously been made by others. The definition of the situation emerged as a group phenomenon and could not be simply characterised as the effect of one or more persons' definitions upon an individual. This is rather like the emergence of group norms discussed with reference to the autokinetic effect above. It is therefore one respect in which behaviour in bystander intervention situations can be seen as social (rather than psychological) in origin.

But Cherry (1995) attacks the conclusions drawn from this research for a further reason. She sees it as fundamentally stripping away and ignoring vital aspects of the social and cultural context of the Kitty Genovese murder, on which it was based. Cherry points out that 'Kitty Genovese and her assailant, Winston

Mosely, were living in a society at a time when its members did little to intervene in violence directed towards women' (p. 19), and she reports how one of the onlookers had been reluctant to get involved in what might have been a lover's quarrel. Furthermore, she argues that 'in 1964 we lived in a world that did not recognise the widespread abuse of women' (p. 21), including spousal abuse, incest and the rape of women by men who were not strangers but familiar to them, and it is widely known that the police have been reluctant to respond to calls for assistance in cases of domestic conflict. Cherry also points out that the murder of Kitty Genovese would probably not have attracted the attention it did if Kitty had not been a white woman living in a respectable, middle-class area. Cherry argues that none of the emergencies used in the laboratory studies of Latané, Darley and their associates included the essential feature of the original crime – an attack by a man on a woman. Instead, this crime became seen as just one example of a larger psychological phenomenon: bystander apathy. In this way she claims that one of the most important means of understanding this crime (that is, in terms of gender/sexual relations and societal norms for these) has been removed from our view, and replaced by a series of situational variables (such as size of group).

Cherry cites later experimental evidence supporting the view that gender relations is the vital factor here rather than situational variables. Borofsky et al. (1971) used a simulated attack scenario and found that men were less likely to intervene in an attack by a man on a woman than in any other gender combination of attacker/victim. Shotland and Straw (1976), also using simulated attacks, found that intervention was more likely when the attacker and victim were perceived as strangers rather than married. Bystander intervention therefore is an example of research where is seems vital to place the phenomena in their full social context of gender, class and race in order to understand them adequately. The meaning of both the emergency itself and of a bystander's intervention is thoroughly suffused with societal assumptions, norms and values, and the important question therefore seems to be how these are communicated between and transmitted to people, becoming part of their own psychology. We should not dismiss the laboratory findings of Latané and Darley, but we should perhaps seek an interpretation of them that acknowledges the field of social expectations, including gender, age, ethnicity, class and so on, present in the experimental context. In similar fashion, the events in Nazi Germany should be seen in their cultural context. It seems unlikely that the Jews would have received markedly fairer or more humane treatment in Germany if Nazi soldiers had been less obedient. The Nazis evidently did not demonstrate the anxiety and tension shown by Milgram's participants, who obviously struggled with the rights and wrongs of inflicting pain on a fellow human being (as of course did many ordinary German people who risked their own lives to help their Jewish neighbours). But the cultural ethos operating in Germany before and during the Second World War was one where Jews were reviled and discriminated against because they were held to be too powerful in business, and, crucially, where notions of racial purity had taken hold and convinced many that non-Aryan races were sub-standard and in need of extermination.

Summary

Social psychology has, rightly, focused upon the nature of social situations when seeking explanations for some human events. However, this chapter has argued that psychological social psychology has tended to follow one of two directions in choosing its methods of enquiry and in formulating its explanations. The first is a return to the self-contained individual and explanations at the level of the individual psyche, as in the case of attitudes (and its associated technology of attitude measurement). The second has been the adherence to a basically behaviouristic and experimental paradigm where variables in the social situation are deemed to cause behavioural outcomes, with or without the mediation of intervening cognitive events such as thoughts or beliefs. Both of these approaches take as their fundamental assumption the self-contained pre-existing and rational individual outlined in Chapter 1.

By re-examining some of the best-known social psychology studies it has been possible to suggest a somewhat different conception of the person and of the origins of social behaviour. Rather than just being acted upon by situational variables, people are curious and actively engaged in forming theories about and making sense of the often ambiguous situations in which they find themselves, and this guides their conduct. A person's conduct is *always* socially situated. It is an illusion to think that we can study behaviour in its pure form, untainted by social considerations. The laboratory itself is a (somewhat bizarre) social situation.

However, the arguments presented above suggest that laboratory experiments usually tell us little about the societal and cultural context of norms and values that gives our conduct its meaning. This is not to say that laboratory experiments tell us nothing, but social influence conceived as a set of situational variables that impact upon the psychology of the individual is perhaps not a helpful way of understanding events in the real world. And if we wish to study those societal and cultural factors, then laboratory experiments are probably not the most useful research tools.

Rather than look to the psyche or to objective features of social situations for our understanding of the person and his or her conduct (which ultimately leaves the psyche intact as a separate realm from the social, just as Descartes believed), we can conceptualise the person in social psychology as an outcrop on the social terrain, where shared, negotiated meanings and situational definitions, norms for appropriate behaviour and *social* attitudes form the landscape. There is no pre-existing individual in this perspective. Instead, the meanings of situations, as well as our own subjectivity, are constituted in those situations in the course of social interaction. It is not that groups either inhibit or encourage particular actions of isolated individuals, but that collectively we construct a definition of the situation that guides and gives meaning to the conduct of all present. This collective construction has been referred to as 'joint action' (Shotter, 1993; see Chapter 6 for a brief account).

Lastly, the meaning of and explanation for a person's behaviour is often only apparent when we see it in the context of shared societal and cultural assumptions and values, and power and structural relations. It could be said that, as persons in Western society, positioned within numerous hierarchies and power relations, our situation is ambiguous. We are at one and the same time drawn toward conformity with groups and obedience to authorities yet exhorted by the ideology of the individual to value independence from these. A truly *social* psychology may need to place such cultural and structural considerations at the centre of its research strategy.

Suggested further reading

Cherry, F. (1995) *The stubborn particulars of social psychology: essays on the research process*. London: Routledge.

Moghaddam, F.M., Taylor, D.M. and Wright, S.C. (1993) *Social psychology in cross-cultural perspective*. New York: W.H. Freeman.

Chapter 3

Role-taking

IN THE LAST CHAPTER, the central argument was that psychological social psychology has presented a conception of the person that artificially divorces it from its social context. The ideology of the self-contained and pre-social individual, originating in the Renaissance and Enlightenment periods, has been a strong influence in the history of this conception (see Chapter 1). I argued for a conception of the person as socially embedded (not simply *affected* by social factors) and consequently for theoretical tools (such as norms) that operate not at the level of the individual but at the level of the collectivity. In the present chapter I will develop this theme by arguing that persons are in important ways defined by their relations to others. The concept of role is central here, and the chapter will focus on the different ways in which this concept can illuminate our understanding of the person.

The power of social roles

Many students of social psychology become familiar with the concept of role through learning about Philip Zimbardo's classic 'Stanford Prison experiment'. Zimbardo was a colleague of Stanley Milgram, and was familiar with his research on obedience. Zimbardo and his co-researchers at Stanford University were interested in understanding the experience of being in prison, both as a prisoner and as a prison guard. Zimbardo had previously been involved in the study of anti-social acts such as vandalism, and was concerned about the apparent ease with which ordinary people could become dehumanised and 'deindividuated' when they are in situations in which they feel anonymous or are able to see others as enemies or less than human. The study, reported in Haney et al. (1973), was carried out in 1971, at a time when there was considerable unrest in US prisons. The controversy and publicity that surrounded the outcome of the study gave Zimbardo a platform on which to speak out against the inhumane conditions in many prisons (e.g. Zimbardo, 1975).

The aim of the study was to have ordinary people carry out the role of prisoner or guard in a realistic prison setting. The basement of a university building was specially converted for the purpose, and the research team advertised for paid volunteers in a local newspaper. The chosen participants were 21 middle-class male college students, all of whom had completed a number of personality tests and were deemed emotionally stable, and who were randomly assigned to their respective roles. To make the situation as realistic as possible, the researchers enlisted the aid of the local police who 'arrested' the prisoners at their homes and subjected them to the normal police arrest procedures at the local station. They were then blindfolded and taken to the university 'prison', where they were stripped, deloused, given a uniform and number, and put into a cell with two other 'prisoners'. The 'guards' were issued with uniforms and told that they were not to use violence and that their job was to maintain control of the prison.

It was intended to run the experiment for two weeks, but it was in fact stopped after five days. The 'guards' quickly became abusive and coercive, and engaged in behaviour calculated to humiliate and dehumanise the 'prisoners'. The 'prisoners' by contrast became depressed and servile. Three of them had to be released during the first four days as they showed extreme traumatic reactions, including hysterical crying and confused thinking. Members of the research team who had experience with real prisons were shocked at the similarity between the behaviour and experience of real prisoners and that of the volunteers. The behaviour of the 'guards' was, if anything, more inhumane than that found in real prisons. Zimbardo (1975) comments 'The majority had indeed become prisoners or guards, no longer able to clearly differentiate between role-playing and self' (p. 268). Drawing on his earlier work on deindividuation, he concluded that ordinary people could be readily induced to perform abusive and anti-social acts if they are put in a situation where they can feel relatively anonymous and where such behaviour is expected of them. He sees the study as confirming the fragility of our individual agency and morality:

> Individual behaviour is largely under the control of social forces and environmental contingencies rather than personality traits, character, will power or other empirically unvalidated constructs. Thus we create an illusion of freedom by attributing more internal control to ourselves, to the individual, than actually exists. We thus underestimate the power and pervasiveness of situational controls over behavior because: a) they are often non-obvious and subtle, b) we can often avoid entering situations where we might be so controlled, c) we label as 'weak' or 'deviant' people in those situations who do behave differently from how we believe we would.
>
> (p. 269)

The power of social roles to produce our behaviour and experience is evidently great, but Zimbardo, in line with the predominant social psychology of his day, frames this power in terms of environmental contingencies and situational controls. Although the self-contained, rational and moral individual is characterised as weak and easily undermined here, the concept of the pre-social individual, at least in principle, is retained in the form of the dichotomy between the individual and the social. The question appears to be 'are we self-determining agents that are capable of making decisions without being unduly influenced by social factors, OR is our behaviour determined by situational factors beyond our control?'. Having shown the apparent ease with which the individual can be undermined, the alternative seems even bleaker: that our behaviour is determined by factors of which we are unaware while we retain the illusion that we have free will.

Zimbardo's claim that *any* ordinary person would behave in the same manner as these prisoners and guards if they were put in that situation enabled him to speak out against imprisonment, since he could argue that it is the nature of the prison system itself and not the pathology of isolated individuals within it that causes inhumanity. But I think to reduce social roles to a set of environmental contingencies is to do a disservice to the richness of the concept as an analytic tool. Craig Haney, one of Zimbardo's co-researchers, also points out that our personal characteristics and beliefs may not be able to guarantee that we always behave as we would hope: 'Individual differences matter very little in the face of an extreme situation ... Institutional settings develop a life of their own independent of the wishes and intentions and purposes of those who run them' (quoted in Maslach, 1997). But the second part of this quote suggests that we perhaps should not look for isolable variables residing in the situation, but should raise our vision to the institutional setting, in other words to the level of the collectivity, to the patterns of relationships existing between people in institutions, sub-cultures and other groups.

Roles as norms and expectations

The idea of role-taking is a long-established one in social psychology, but it is the tradition of sociological social psychology that has made most use of it, and it is this conception of role-taking that I will argue has most to offer us. Role-taking is a key concept in the area of sociological social psychology known as symbolic interactionism, which began life with the works of George Mead early in the twentieth century (see Chapter 1). The part of the concept that has more recently been widely taken up is the aspect of roles that embodies normative prescriptions for our conduct. Ralph Linton, a cultural anthropologist, introduced social psychologists to the notion of social status as an explanatory concept, and 'role expectations' was a related concept introduced by him and other social anthropologists in the 1930s. But it is important to realise that the original concept of role-taking (and role-making) introduced by Mead was more sophisticated than this. For the purposes of this chapter, we will begin with the simpler 'roles as social expectations' concept, and then move on to role-taking as it was and is conceptualised by symbolic interactionists.

Linton (1945) introduced the 'status-role' concept. In any society, people occupy status positions in numerous aspects of their social structure. They may occupy status positions given by their sex, their age, their occupation, their membership of kinship and friendship groups or exclusive clubs and so on. Each of these statuses is a description of the person's position in their society relative to other persons, and each brings with it a set of prescriptions for how a person of that status should behave: their role. Roles refer to the norms and expectations attached to a particular status in society. Of course the different statuses that we occupy are not all salient or active for us at the same time, and therefore the role behaviours that we are called upon to perform will vary too. When we are at home with our families, the roles of father, aunt or neighbour will be prominent, and when we are at work the roles of employee, boss or workmate will take their place and our family roles will become latent.

Roles give us a much wider conception of our potential conduct than could a number of norms acquired separately. For example, an alien being visiting Earth in the 1950s and having landed in Britain or the USA might learn that it is normative for females to wear make-up and care for children, and that it is normative for men to drink beer and play sport. But once the alien had grasped the concept of gender roles it would be in a much better position to anticipate and understand a whole variety of other female and male behaviours that fell within the remit of femininity and masculinity. According to Linton, our statuses are ascribed to us by society but the roles attached to them have to be learned by us. So a good deal of our inculcation into society involves learning the roles attached to the statuses we have been ascribed. Interestingly, Linton argues that the rapid and fundamental changes taking place in modern societies, including advances in technology and increased social and geographical mobility, means that the system of statuses and roles that we have inherited from earlier generations is breaking down. This means that we can increasingly expect to find ourselves in situations where we are unsure of our status and role or those of others, leading to uncertainties, frustrations and disappointments in our dealings with each other. With respect to the example above, an alien landing in Britain or the USA today may find it much harder to work out what role behaviours are currently expected of women and men (some would argue that you don't need to be an alien to experience this difficulty).

In psychological social psychology, the concept of role has been used to explain the behaviour of research participants. Here, role is understood not so much in terms of broad and relatively stable social statuses (sex, age etc.) but in terms of the more localised and transient positions we may be called upon to occupy, like the role of the experimental subject. For example Orne (1971) demonstrated that subjects instructed to behave as if they were hypnotised responded to suggestions in a manner consistent with the popular understanding of what it means to be hypnotised and their behaviour was often hard to distinguish from that of real hypnotised subjects. Similarly, Haney et al. (1973) saw the behaviour of their prisoners and guards as an outcome of the roles they had adopted, but these roles involved more than responding to a set of situational demands (see Chapter 2). In a letter to the American Psychologist in 1975, De Jong argues against the view that the participants in the Stanford Prison Experiment were responding to powerful demand characteristics in the experimental situation, including the acting out of common prison stereotypes. De Jong points out that responding to demand characteristics could hardly produce the distress and depression characteristic of the prisoners, and that the behaviour of the guards went far beyond what might have been construed as expected of them. De Jong goes on to argue that the participants were indeed in a sense acting out common stereotypes in their role-playing, and that this in fact makes them indistinguishable from real prisoners and guards:

> . . . guards in a real penitentiary could also be said to be 'playing a role' when they first begin their jobs. Like the guards in the prison study, real guards are given little or no training. Beyond what they have seen in films or heard from the more experienced guards, they really do not know what to expect. Just like the guards in the prison study, they only know that they must be 'tough' with the prisoners in order to maintain order. In what way, then, is the subsequent behaviour of the guards in the study any less 'real' than the behaviour of novice guards in actual penitentiaries?
>
> (p. 272)

Role-playing as enactment

One of the issues behind this debate seems to be about the status of role-playing as inauthentic or pretence. Playing a role is seen as quite different from 'being yourself'. Zimbardo talks of his volunteers being no longer able 'to differentiate between role-playing and self'. But De Jong's letter highlights an important issue about role-playing in general. When we undertake new duties and responsibilities in life, or acquire new statuses, say through a change of job, a promotion, becoming a parent or getting a divorce, for a while it can feel as though we are just acting out a role. Our behaviour can feel inauthentic or fake to us. When I first became a lecturer my students were not necessarily aware that I was a newcomer to the job. For some time I was aware of a strong sense of just putting on an act, and I was convinced that students would inevitably guess that I wasn't a 'real' lecturer. But as I gained more experience and watched other lecturers in action these feelings diminished and then disappeared. I had become a lecturer. But to say that at first I was role-playing and that later I was being myself doesn't make sense. I was and am in important ways both being myself and playing a role. This is particularly striking when we consider roles such as parent, friend or neighbour. No-one would argue with the claim that these roles demand quite different behaviours of us, but it seems ludicrous to suggest that our parenting, friendship or neighbourliness is a mere pretence. We are still ourselves when in all of these roles.

The distinction between self and role is therefore often not a useful one, because it prevents us from fully using the concept of role to understand our sense of self, the sense of self that is authentic and not 'fake'. Even the profession of acting itself is often misconceived as needing a talent for pretending to be something you are not. For the actor, the process of 'getting into role' is not one of carefully covering up their real self with a fake exterior. The convincing performance requires that the actor find some aspect of themselves that can be fleshed out and elaborated in the role they must play. The convincing actor is therefore not an impostor but someone who is particularly able to imaginatively extend and build upon some aspect of their own existing experience and behaviour and to temporarily live out their construction. We can also assume that some people, like some actors, might have better role-playing skills, leading to more convincing performances. Of course the script and the props are helpful too. If you want to be a convincing villain, it helps if you are provided with cloak and dagger and given lines to speak that are suitably menacing. This is just what happened to the Stanford participants; the props and costumes were provided in the form of prison uniforms and cells, and the script was available to all in the form of culturally shared assumptions about the behaviour of prisoners and guards. It is important to recognise that this notion of role is not as prescriptive (and therefore deterministic) as it might seem. When we act out roles, follow scripts and use props we do so in a manner similar to that of the 'method' actor,* whose precise words are neither planned nor written down but improvised in the course of the enactment. The script exists as a number of potential variations on a theme of 'the kind of thing this character would say in this kind of situation'.

The power of enactment in bringing about personal change was recognised by George Kelly, a psychotherapist who developed the theory of personal constructs (1955). Kelly devised a form of therapy that he called 'fixed role'. Here, the therapist writes a character sketch for the client, including examples of things the character might do or say, how they react to situations and what they might think or feel. The character sketch is intended to incorporate some aspects of the client's current way of thinking and behaving, but also includes new or alternative forms of conduct. The client is asked to live out this role in his or her daily life for a fixed period, perhaps a few days or weeks. The point of the exercise for the client, who may desperately wish to change but be afraid of what they might become, is to see themselves in a new light and to experience their social world from a different vantage point without a commitment to 'buy' the new identity. The important point is that, just as in becoming a lecturer or a prison guard, adopting unaccustomed ways of behaving and speaking (both involved in taking on a strange role) is often the first step to changing who you are. It is sometimes claimed that women make good carers because they are more nurturant than men, or that men succeed in business because they are ambitious. However, putting aside all other factors (such as opportunities and discrimination) we might better claim that women are nurturant because they are often involved in caring roles and that men are ambitious because their work roles are structured by career ladders. We should not be surprised to find a similarity between people who have a similar position and role in society or in an

---

* So-called 'method' acting was originated by the Russian actor and director Konstantin Stanislavsky in the 1920s, and later taken up in the USA. Stanislavsky rejected the declamatory style of acting in favour of a more realistic approach concentrating on the psychological development of a character rather than the technical side of its presentation.

institution, and we should not expect something that we call a person's real self to transcend the roles they play.

It is sometimes said 'you are what you eat'. In the present context, we can say 'you are what you do'; we become the roles we play. This only seems an extreme or dangerous statement if we try to retain our traditional concept of the self-contained, pre-social individual. It is this concept that leads us to distinguish between self and role and to then relegate the latter to the realm of pretence (the self being seen as real by comparison with role). Of course there are occasions when we feel uncomfortable in a role that is demanded of us, and we may even take steps to signal to other people that what they are seeing in our role-playing is not the 'real me' (termed 'role distancing' by Goffman, 1961). People do not passively and unreflectively act out the roles that are given them. The sense of who they are, their self-concept, will affect the ease with which they feel able to don a particular role. Nevertheless, we should beware of explaining such occasions in terms of a conflict between the demands of a socially bestowed role and a pre-existing essential self. Our self-concept may be just as socially derived as the roles we adopt, so that, although self and role are often indistinguishable and can be seen to merge into each other, this does not mean that we have to accept a view of the person that is deterministic. To say that the person is a product of social factors (like norms and roles) is just as deterministic as saying that the person is a product of pre-existing genetic material and personality traits. Both views lead us back into the dualist vision of the individual (internal, subjective) and society (external, objective) as separate realms, as in the Cartesian conception of the person (see Chapter 1). An important and fundamental difference between psychological social psychology on the one hand and sociological social psychology and more recent European developments (see Chapter 5) on the other is the refusal of the latter to accept this dualism, and the development of conceptions of the person where society and the individual are inseparable. Symbolic interactionism is one such theory, and its treatment of role extends and goes beyond the idea of roles as sets of expectations that accompany social statuses.

Taking the role of the other

Symbolic interactionism turns on its head the conventional psychological conception of the relationship between the individual and society. Psychology's individual pre-exists society. This individual is endowed with a mind which is capable of reflecting upon the outside world and upon the individual's experience of this. It also has a self which it can reflect upon with its mind. Language is seen as a tool that makes it possible for the reflections of mind to become externalised and available to the outside world. Thus through language the individual is able to communicate the contents of its mind, its reflections on the world and itself. In this conception, both the mind and the self are assumed to already exist and make it possible for individuals to communicate with each other and have meaningful interaction – the rudiments of any society.

Symbolic interactionism is a radical challenge to this view. It argues that 'society and individuals are the product of interaction (communication) between people and that this interaction takes place through the use of symbols which have meaning for the individuals involved' (Flory, 2000). Both mind (our capacity for consciousness, for reflection upon our experience) and self are seen as made possible by and emerging from the processes of social interaction and language use. Central components of the person in this form of social psychology are therefore seen as socially contingent: they depend upon meaningful social interaction for their development in the person. We cannot think about or reflect upon our experience (this is what is meant by mind) until we are able to symbolically represent events to ourselves through language. And we cannot acquire language without engaging in social interaction. As babies, we are born already capable of rudimentary interaction. Babies engage in turn-taking and imitation games with their caregivers (Schaffer, 1977; Kaye, 1982). This in itself does not constitute mind: a baby is not yet capable of reflecting upon this interaction. But this rudimentary interaction takes the same structural form as a conversation and imitation is 'a process on the verge of putting oneself mentally in the place of others and acting towards them on the basis of under-standing their situation' (Ashworth, 1979, p. 95). Furthermore, the baby's part in this 'conversation', its actions, *becomes* mean-ingful through the way the caregiver responds. Adults and older children respond to a baby *as if* its actions were already mean-ingful, and in this way both baby and caregivers come to mutually define certain actions as having particular meanings. At this point in its development, the child is engaged in what Mead (1934) termed a 'conversation of gestures'. As the child's cognitive capac-ities increase, it becomes able to replace these gestures with symbols – words. Through the continued process of social inter-action, the child is able to move away from this conversation of gestures and participate in its society's system of shared symbols and their meanings (language). Language is therefore a kind of covert social interaction, a conversation of gestures carried out privately through the use of symbols. At this point, the child has become capable of truly reflecting upon and representing both the world and its own actions to itself and others. It has acquired both mind and self.

For symbolic interactionism it is therefore social relation-ships that provide the basis for the development of the person. This development also depends upon our natural capacity to search for and assign meaning to events, to interpret them. But there is something more to be said before we have adequately characterised the human mind in symbolic interactionist terms. It is not simply that we assign meaning to our actions and to those of other people. Human interaction as we would recognise it also demands that we have some conception of the meaning that our actions hold for others, and that we know that they will know that we have such a conception. Meaningful human social inter-action is distinguished by this characteristic: we are able to imaginatively anticipate the effects of our actions on others and act accordingly. This is a result of our ability to represent actions through our system of shared meanings. When we interact through gestures, and later through language, we know that a gesture or word has the same meaning for others as it has for us. We there-fore have a kind of access to the minds of others; we can anticipate the meaning that our actions have for them because of the meaning they have for us. We can therefore represent to ourselves what would happen *if* we were to undertake a certain course of action. We are able to consider alternative courses of possible action, which is one way of describing agency. Mead saw this capacity as what separates the meaningful interaction of humans from the meaningful interaction of other animals (leaving aside the debate about whether some species have a consciousness or language that is comparable to that of humans). Ashworth (1979) illustrates this with an example using dogs. He demonstrates that although dogs may be involved in meaningful interaction, it is not interaction in the human sense:

> A dog does not imagine what response its gesturing will bring forth in the other dog. To bring this idea about more clearly: suppose a team of dogs was taught to play a game akin to football – what sort of performance would they put up? Mead would say that animals would certainly have no tactical sense. Behaviour like passing a dummy ball would be impossible, because it requires the player to imagine the response that a gesture will bring out, and then act in a way deliberately to mislead. To imagine means to be able to understand the role expectations of the other. This dogs cannot do, Mead claims.
>
> Dog footballers would merely run all over the pitch – the stimulus provided by the behaviour of the one dog calling forth a relatively automatic response in the others.
>
> (p. 9)

Our ability to imagine and act upon the meanings that we anticipate that our actions will hold for others was termed by Mead 'taking the role of the other'. This means that human beings acquire the ability, through their use of significant symbols as described above, to stand in each other's shoes and view the world (and each other) through each other's eyes. Our role in a situation is therefore always a function of the roles of others. The term role therefore describes one's social situation relative to other people at any moment. It is therefore less likely to refer to ascribed social statuses (although it encompasses these) than to the part one plays in a given situation. This conception of role extends the idea of role as social statuses because it emphasises the reciprocity of roles. It requires you to see yourself and your conduct through the eyes of other people. Carrying out a role not only involves a knowledge of what is expected of you, but also requires an appreciation of how your role dovetails with that of others in your current social situation. Taking the role of the other is what enables us to have any kind of meaningful social interaction, from an argument to a game of tennis. Both require that we can anticipate what our conduct will mean to the other.

Symbolic interactionism therefore places role-taking at the very heart of what it means to be a person, and this concept of role must always involve at least two people; it is not possible for a role, in the symbolic interactionist sense, to exist simply as a property of a lone individual. A consequence of this reciprocity is that our ability to carry out our own role depends upon the ability and preparedness of others in the situation to carry out theirs:

> A role cannot exist without one or more relevant other-roles toward which it is oriented. The role of 'father' makes no sense without the role of child; it can be defined as a pattern of behaviour only in relation to the pattern of behaviour of a child. The role of the compromiser can exist only to the extent that others in a group are playing the role of antagonists. The role of hero is distinguished from the role of the foolhardy only by the role of the actor's real or imaginary audience ... This role reciprocity provides a generalised explanation for changed behaviour. A change in one's own role reflects a changed assessment or perception of the role of relevant others. Interaction is always a *tentative* process, a process of continuously testing the conception one has of the role of the other. The response of the other serves to reinforce or to challenge this conception. The product of the testing process is the stabilisation or the modification of one's own role.

> (Turner, 1962, p. 23, italics in original)

Thus, the roles we adopt, and the selfhood that is implicated by them, are fragile since they depend upon the co-operation of others to play their requisite parts. To some degree, then, roles and selfhood are socially negotiated productions. The concept of negotiation also brings with it the possibility that we have some degree of choice in the roles we adopt in interaction. An example of the negotiation of roles is found in a study by Davis (1961), reported in Jackson (1988):

> Davis (1961) observed how a physiotherapist tried to convert a person with a temporary physical handicap into a *patient*. The therapist emphasized the disability's seriousness, to persuade the person to relinquish 'normal' roles usually played in favor of total patienthood. The person responded by emphasizing the handicap's temporary character and the imminent prospect of recovery. The person attempted to establish friendly relations by providing personal details about self, asking the therapist personal questions, extending social invitations and in other ways attempting to avoid becoming 'only' a patient. The therapist could not play a completely professional role unless the person became a complete patient, however, so that offers of friendship and intimacy were rejected. But the therapist still could not afford to be viewed as cold and distant by either patient or colleagues. A 'distant cordiality' was maintained as a role relationship emerged from the negotiation.
>
> (pp. 124–125, italics in original)

In order to carry out a role within any social situation, a person must first have some conception of what kind of situation is at hand, since different situations contain different potential roles for participants. The person must therefore define the situation. The definition of the situation is a key concept for symbolic interactionism. The definition of the situation as a factor in producing social behaviour has already been discussed in Chapter 2. People can be expected to behave differently according to whether they define a situation as, for example, 'a chat with a friend' or 'a consultation with a therapist'. But the definition of the situation as it is used in psychology has a one-sided, intra-psychic character. It appears as a cognitive quality of the individual, rather like an attitude or opinion, and is represented as a discrete event; the individual takes a view on 'what is going on here' and then acts accordingly. For symbolic interactionism, situations can only ever be mutually defined by the participants involved in them. Furthermore, this definition is constantly under production by all parties, constantly monitored and liable to breakdown. Because of the reciprocal nature of roles, no-one can be sure of acting appropriately or of being allowed to play a particular role unless all share the same definition of the situation. This does not mean that all parties in an interaction somehow mysteriously find themselves agreeing about 'what is going on here'. There may be conflicting definitions in operation. But if one's own definition is at odds with that of other participants, this will necessarily have implications for the viability of the roles that they are attempting to play. Thus there will then usually ensue a good deal of effort directed at establishing and maintaining a mutually agreed or negotiated definition, including the use of role-distancing described earlier. The fundamental point that symbolic interactionism is making is that people 'have a grasp of the *structure* of situations' (Hewitt, 1988, p. 79). If the structure of a situation is not clear to us, that is, we are not sure how to define it and our role in it vis-à-vis others is therefore ambiguous, we set about creating a structure:

> Thus, if we encounter a situation in which it is not clear who occupies what positions and plays what roles, we turn our attention to figuring out these matters. We decide who around us has authority over us, to whom we are supposed to address a question, as well as who we are in the eyes of others. And if we find ourselves in a situation that is so ambiguous that there is no structure to it, we create one. A newly formed group, for example, may be quite undifferentiated, but before long some people become leaders and others followers, some are active and some are not, some take on this task and others that one. In short, we look for structure, and where we do not find it, we create it.
>
> (Hewitt, 1988, p. 80)

But roles and the definition of the situation exist in a chicken-and-egg relationship, so that, although our definition of the situation indicates to us our possible role and its attendant expectations, we also define the situation through our observation of the roles apparently adopted by others. We ourselves help to create that definition through our own adoption of certain postures, in the way we present ourselves – through the role we claim for ourselves in that interaction. A situation is therefore necessarily a socially negotiated event; it cannot exist simply at the level of an individual's psychology. Roles, too, are never simply prescribed and then enacted. Symbolic interactionism refers to role-*making* as well as role-*taking* to emphasise the fluidity and adaptability of the roles we play:

> roles provide us with an organising framework that we can use to make a performance that will meet the needs of a particular situation . . . . Role-making thus becomes a very self-conscious activity in which the person is creatively engaged in making an appropriate role performance, not a blind activity in which a script is routinely enacted.
>
> (Hewitt, 1988, p. 83)

Taking the role of the other places social interaction at the very centre of what it means to be a person. It is social interaction, according to symbolic interactionism, that gives us mind or consciousness and enables us to acquire language and to communicate with each other, and to develop a sense of who we are, our self. But this view requires that we reject the individual/society and self/role dualisms characteristic of psychological social psychology. If we do this, we find that the territory that psychology has covered for most of the last century becomes curiously relocated. The self is no longer the private property of the individual, located in cognitive structures, genetic material or personality traits but a fragile and fluid construction negotiated in partnership with others in social interaction. The implicit dualisms of deep vs. surface and real vs. pretence have characterised psychology's conception of the relation between the individual and society, such that psychic structures are seen as deeper, more real and more truthful or authentic than social roles. These dichotomies must also be rejected if we take on board a symbolic interactionist perspective. The social (rather than the psychological) becomes primary, in that it is society (in the form of social interaction) that makes possible our personhood, and our psychology thus becomes contingent rather than pre-existent. And the person becomes co-terminous with his or her appearance in the social realm: there is no real self lurking behind a pretended role. Ultimately, this will lead us to question to what extent we can in fact usefully operate a distinction between the psychological and the social.

Role-taking as self-presentation

The fact that we find it extraordinarily difficult to understand and accept such a claim is shown in the criticisms that have been levelled at the ideas of one of the few Symbolic Interactionists generally known to psychologists – Erving Goffman. As a sociologist, Goffman gave uncharacteristically little attention to social structure in his work. His focus was firmly on social interaction, and in particular upon how people create and manage the impressions they make on others – how they present themselves. Goffman (1959) argued that in all our social encounters we are fundamentally concerned with self-presentation, and that indeed this necessarily must be so. In the course of many brief social encounters we are simply not in a position to know a person's motives or their true feelings, to verify their claims about their status or background or to know whether they will eventually betray our trust. We must take people on faith and do what we can to gain an impression of them from the way they conduct or express themselves. Goffman is therefore signalling that this self-presentation is in no way trivial; it is a widespread and crucial aspect of social life. In every social encounter, we are engaged in making an implicit claim to be a particular kind of person or to occupy a particular role in that situation, and the impression that we make on others of course may or may not be the one we are trying to achieve. Our performances are susceptible to disruption by accident, sabotage or inexperience, so that our claim may become discredited in the course of our performance, and this is what, according to Goffman, constitutes embarrassment. In fact, so fragile are these impressions that we must constantly ward off disaster by monitoring our performance and taking precautions to avoid or otherwise deal with potential discrediting events we see on the horizon. For their part, the members of our audience help us along by taking steps to preserve the definition of the situation that we are trying to project – what we normally refer to as tact. The other people making up our audience can, by their own conduct, either legitimate or reject our claim to be a certain kind of person, and Goffman argues that this is done by carefully monitoring the match or mis-match between what we 'give' (the things we say or do to create an impression) and what we 'give off' (our body language, our general demeanour – the communicative aspects of our conduct that are harder for us to control and manipulate). The creation and maintenance of impressions is therefore a two-way street.

For Goffman, then, the roles we play and our 'presentation of self' to others forms a major daily enterprise in social life. Our attempts to do this and to maintain 'face' are so important that disruptions and their accompanying embarrassments are a recurring theme in our humour and our dreams. We may argue that role-playing is something that we have to engage in on certain kinds of social occasions where it is necessary to pass ourselves off as certain kinds of people, to make a good impression, but that the rest of the time we are surely just being ourselves. Radley (1991), however, points out that even in the most transient and insignificant of our social encounters we are defining the situation and claiming a character for ourselves, and that this is made evident when the role expectations implicit in the encounter are not met:

> Consider buying a loaf of bread in a baker's shop. Here is a very simple exchange in which presenting oneself as a special kind of person is hardly the reason for its happening

– you want to buy some bread! Further consideration will show, however, that there is a variety of ways in which we can ask for a loaf, in which the assistant can acknowledge our request and deal with the transaction. If we are polite and friendly in our manner, and then are dealt with in an abrupt and offhand manner, we feel slighted. It is not that we needed to claim that we are 'really nice people', but that we treated the assistant and the situation in a certain way and expected to be treated in a manner consistent with that claim.

(Radley, 1991, p. 19)

Because of his emphasis upon impression-management in everyday life, Goffman has been interpreted as suggesting that social life is little more than a complex sham, where people are busily engaged in concealing their real motives and their true disposition by skilled performances. While we know that it is true that we sometimes actively and consciously strive to create a particular kind of impression, we nevertheless feel that this just isn't an accurate description of many of our social encounters, where we feel that we are just being ourselves. But this is to misunderstand the assumption at the heart of Goffman's work, which is a rejection of the distinction between self and role. For Goffman, the presentation of self does not mean that we present to an external world a pre-existing, internal self. The presentation is all there is. This *is* the self:

> To *be* a given kind of person, then, is not merely to possess the required attributes, but also to sustain the standards of conduct and appearance that one's social grouping attaches thereto. The unthinking ease with which performers consistently carry off such standard-maintaining routines does not deny that a performance has occurred, merely that the participants have been aware of it.
>
> (Goffman, 1959, p. 65, italics in original)

This absolutely does not mean that the self is superficial and fake. It means that we have to reject the self-role and superficial–deep dualisms and accept that what we call the self might be something that is constantly negotiated, claimed and legitimated or denied, in the course of social interaction. Goffman's account also gives the person agency, since there must be a reflective actor who claims roles and defines situations, who constantly monitors and reflects upon their own and others' performances, and who tries to distance themself from other roles, and who generally orchestrates the performance that is their presentation of self. He distinguishes between the person as 'character', the self that is manufactured during social encounters, and the person as 'performer', who learns a 'part', has hopes and aspirations for their performances, and exercises tact with respect to the performances of others.

Goffman's view of social interaction also puts an interesting spin on our emotional life. He gives a good deal of attention to embarrassment (e.g. Goffman, 1967), which is surely the most social of emotions. We can imagine feeling sad, euphoric or jealous without the physical presence of other people. But the experience of embarrassment usually requires a social situation, and Goffman sees it as what happens when performers realise that one of them has been unable to carry off their role or fulfil their claim to be a particular kind of person. His analysis neatly explains why it is that we often feel embarrassed for someone who has lost face in an interaction. Since interactants are always busily engaged in maintaining their negotiated definition of the situation, so that each may play their role, if one person's role becomes invalidated this throws the whole situation into question. The interaction may grind to a halt as the participants struggle to save their definition of the situation or hastily construct a new one. All participants share in the embarrassment because their own roles in the situation are no longer viable. For example, when attending conferences academics are accustomed to sitting in lecture halls, listening with quiet attention to presentations by persons who (by virtue of being invited or permitted to speak) are defined as being experts in their field. The role of the speaker must therefore be carefully performed so as to legitimate their implicit claim to be a person worth listening to. The role of audience members is to listen attentively, ask relevant or even challenging questions, and generally show that they have understood the presentation. But what happens if the speaker finds that he or she has forgotten the details of the theory or research study he or she set out to explain, becomes flustered and apolgises? What if a member of the audience shows, by the nature of their question, that they have misunderstood the whole point of the speaker's argument? In either case, both speaker and audience become embarrassed because their implicit and mutual roles in the situation have suddenly become untenable. Embarrassment is a constant threat to 'face' because one of the roles we are very frequently called upon to perform is that of the competent social actor. So that when we say the wrong thing, unintentionally insult someone, forget a name and so on, we are invalidating our claim to that role.

If we understand embarrassment in this way, we can also begin to see related forms of social anxiety in a new light. Many people feel shy in some social situations, and some experience intense anxiety at the thought of, say, speaking in public or meeting new people. Psychology has tended to regard such people as either possessing a pathologically retiring nature (the personality trait view) or as having failed to acquire a basic understanding of the rules of social interaction (the social skills view). But it could be said that such people have a more acute than usual perception of the intricacies of social interactions, and are able to pick up very subtle cues that convince them that the interaction is about to founder and embarrassment is just around the corner. The person who is seen as socially unskilled may have a very good understanding of the rules of social interaction (making eye contact, taking turns etc.) but be unable to put them into practice because they fear that their performance of the role they are claiming, or that of 'competent social actor', will not be convincing to others. Indeed, those truly without social skills may be better characterised as failing to notice the social blunders of themselves or others. The person who is unaware that they speak too loudly or stand too close in conversation may be risible or discomfiting, but they are not an embarrassment to themselves or others. As Radley (1991) points out, the social skills metaphor often blinds us to the fact that acceptable social performance is under the regulation of a variety of norms and values. For example, a person's physical build or appearance may lie outside of the prescribed norms for their gender, so that they feel unable to legitimately claim an appropriate gender role for themselves in an interaction.

Other emotions, too, are only felt in the presence or implied presence of others. Humiliation and shame are 'social emotions' in the same way, and the distinctions that we make between embarrassment, humiliation and shame are determined primarily by the nature of the particular social rule that has been infringed on any occasion. So that rather than think of (at least some) emotions as essentially private events belonging to our psychology, we may think of them as social by definition, originating and existing in the social realm, between people. In fact, the arguments presented in this chapter together constitute a very different conception of the person than that offered by traditional psychological social psychology. Large tracts of what is normally regarded as psychological territory, existing prior to society and the property of the individual, may instead be thought of as contingent upon social relations and existing between people in their interactions. To the extent that the self encompasses our character, our ways of behaving and emotional reactions then these parts of our psychology can legitimately be seen as being produced and maintained in the course of daily social life.

Summary

Whether we are speaking about roles as ascribed statuses carrying expectations or roles as positions in interactions, using the concept to understand social behaviour lifts the origins of that behaviour out of the realm of intra-psychic psychology and places it in the realm of the social. Roles cannot be understood simply as a property of a person's psyche, although taking on a role is clearly experienced in all the ways we would acknowledge as psychological: behavioural, cognitive and emotional. But role is a concept that operates at the level of the collectivity (or at the level of the dyad at the very least) and not at the level of the individual. Furthermore, its location is in social situations or episodes, not de-contextualised fragments of behaviour.

If we hold in abeyance our belief in the pre-existent and pre-social individual, we can make way for a vision of the person in which who we are emerges through the adoption of roles during social interaction. The equating of self with role, however, only works if we abandon dichotomies such as real vs. pretend, surface vs. deep and, ultimately, individual vs. social. Once we do this, we need no longer be troubled by the idea that people are social impostors or that they are unduly influenced by variables in the social situation. We also need not be unduly concerned about free will and determinism. To say that people are produced in the course of social interaction in no way means that they are *determined* by social factors. As we have seen, there is plenty of room for disagreement and conflict over definitions of the situation and our place in them, and the resolution of these by negotiation. The socially contingent person therefore is not without agency.

Suggested further reading

Ashworth, P.D. (1979) *Social interaction and consciousness*. Chichester: Wiley.

George's Page: the Mead Project website. URL http://paradigm.soci. brocku.ca/~lward/default.html

Chapter 4

Groups
and the
social self

I N CHAPTER THREE, I ARGUED that the kind
of person one is and one's sense of that personhood, one's sense of self, is socially derived.
The chapter focused on role-taking and role-
making to illustrate this. In the present chapter I
want to continue with this argument, showing
how one's identity, the sense of 'who I am', is
greatly dependent upon the groups and social categories of various kinds of which one is a member.
Such groups may be formal, such as clubs and
associations, or they may be kinship and friendship networks, or sub-cultures. They may be
groups to which we have chosen to belong, categories of people to which we belong by virtue of
possessing some personal attribute, or groups
to which we aspire. And the identities conferred
on us by being a member of these groups may be
desired, welcomed or resisted by us. But the common factor uniting all these identities is that they

are socially bestowed. They do not arise as a consequence of psychological qualities residing within us but of social processes operating between us and other people. In discussing these processes, I will draw upon both 'psychological' social psychology as well as the 'sociological' social psychology of symbolic interactionism. Both of these approaches, in different ways, have contributed to our understanding of the extraordinary power of social groups to shape our personhood.

Identity and groups

The study of groups in the early days of social psychology focused upon the fear that the group or crowd context could undermine the rationality and morality of the individual. This was at the root of Le Bon's concept of 'group mind' (see Chapter 1) and informed much of the later study of 'social influence'. According to Parker (1989) 'The prospect of crowd phenomena seizing individual minds haunted American social psychologists' (p. 36) and 'Opposition to the crowd and attempts to safeguard individual autonomy were held together by the method of laboratory experimentation. Such a method produced its own mechanistic caricature of the rational individual . . .' (p. 37). Parker sees F.H. Allport's insistence upon the pre-existing individual, whose 'original nature' was merely modified by social factors that could be discovered by experimentation, as partly fuelled by a fear that Le Bon may be right and a consequent desire to prove him wrong. Le Bon's theory apparently arose from his witnessing terrifying episodes of crowd behaviour at the time of the Paris Commune in 1871, and although many aspects of his 'group mind' theory have since been discredited (he claimed that the crowd member is reduced to the activities of the spinal cord and is in a state of evolutionary regression) his view that crowd members become anonymous and lose their identity remained influential, for example in Zimbardo's (1969) concept of 'deindividuation'. The flavour of the concept is evident from the title of this work: 'The human choice: individuation, reason and order versus deindividuation, impulse and chaos'.

However, Brown (1988a) argues that the emphasis on the negative outcomes of group membership is misplaced, and that instead of leading us to *lose* our identity and become an anonymous crowd member, the crowd can provide us with a powerful *sense* of identity. For example, Reicher (1984) studied a riot in Bristol, England, which involved clashes between the police and members of the mainly black local community. He found that, rather than losing their identities, some of the 'rioters' developed a keen pride in their community through their actions. Whatever else may be happening, the solidarity evidenced in crowds where there is a common purpose or desire, whether the event is a political demonstration or a football match, surely strengthens rather than reduces salient aspects of our identity. The fan of Manchester United or the Washington Redskins may have numerous strands to their identity, but during a game their identity as 'supporter' and all that implies come to the fore, so that the person's aims and desires literally become identified with those of the team.

Intergroup conflict

Much of the research that has contributed to our understanding of social identity has come from the study of intergroup conflict, and includes both experimental and field studies. Among the most famous of these were the 'Robbers' Cave' studies carried out by Muzafer Sherif and his co-workers in the 1950s. The Robbers' Cave was a State Park in a mountainous area of SE Oklahoma, containing a 260-acre Boy Scouts of America camp. Sherif argued that the violent behaviour of some people in groups is not explained by a 'herd instinct', as suggested by Le Bon's theory, but by the presence of incompatible goals. Where the aims of one's own group (the 'in-group') can only be realised at the expense of those of the other group (the 'out-group'), we can expect conflict.

Sherif took advantage of the custom of middle-class families to send their sons to summer camps for several weeks. In each of his studies of intergroup relations, the participants were the twenty or so young boys attending the camp (who had been

81

the twenty or so young boys attending the camp (who had been screened and selected by Sherif), the camp organisers being Sherif and his co-workers. Sherif was interested not only in intergroup conflict but also in how the status and role of individual boys within the group changed over time. He documented the day-to-day reactions of the boys to their situation, and his report (Sherif *et al.*, 1961) describes their behaviour in colourful detail. Although the researchers' observations were anecdotal rather than systematic, the ebb and flow of the boys' allegiances to their groups is vividly illustrated.

The aim of the research was to artificially create two groups, to foster competition and conflict between them, and to observe the changing relations between the groups as the researchers introduced strategies aimed at conflict reduction. In the first stage of the research, 'group formation', the boys were randomly assigned to one of two groups (in one of the studies the groups called themselves the 'Rattlers' and the 'Eagles'), and were engaged in their own, separate activities. Sherif observed that each group quickly developed its own structure, norms and sub-culture. In the second stage, 'intergroup competition', a number of competitive situations were introduced, for example a softball game or a tug-of-war, where the two groups were pitted against each other. At this stage, there was a clear favouritism for members of each boy's own group and the nature of intergroup relations took on a different character, becoming much more hostile and involving the creation of stereotypes, name-calling and sometimes physical aggression. In the final stage, 'conflict reduction', a series of 'crises' were manufactured which required boys from both groups to act co-operatively in order to secure resources vital to all of them. For example, while the boys were on a camping trip some distance from their base, a truck that was to be used to go shopping for food would not start (it had of course been sabotaged by the researchers), and had to be pulled along by all the boys until it did. Sherif noticed that with each successive co-operative venture, the intergroup hostility and negative attitudes decreased, and at the end of the holiday the boys elected to travel home on their buses in mixed groups. The fact that the groups in Sherif's studies were sometimes in conflict but worked in co-operation at other times, depending upon whether their goals were compatible, supported his theory and put in doubt the 'herd instinct' view of group influence, although it is of course debatable as to how far 'groups' and 'crowds' can be considered similar.

The aim of these studies was explicitly an examination of intergroup conflict, and there is some question about the extent to which the competitiveness engendered in these boys is generalisable to other cultures (Moghaddam et al., 1993). Nevertheless, the general finding that groups that perceive themselves to be in competition with each other tend to favour their own in-group has been demonstrated in both laboratory and naturalistic studies (see Brown, 1988b). For our purposes what is important is the ease and strength with which we appear to derive our identity from group membership. The boys in Sherif's studies were not given incentives to develop a cohesive group identity: it happened 'naturally' on being assigned to one group or the other. Indeed, where some of the boys had developed a friendship on the way to the camp, the friends were subsequently assigned to different groups. Their early relationships did not prevent the boys from acting towards their former friends in just the same way as toward any other 'out-group' member. Much effort and imagination went into thinking up group symbols, names and norms of appropriate behaviour. It seems that it was necessary to clearly establish the meaning and significance of being a 'Rattler' or an 'Eagle'. Despite some ethical reservations about these studies (consent, debriefing and so on) they have considerable ecological validity: the boys were engaged in activities and circumstances very like those at any typical boys' camp. The strength and rapidity with which group identities were formed suggests the importance of these in our everyday lives. These boys were temporarily removed from all their usual social groups – their families, schools and friends. Their customary landmarks for their sense of self were missing, and it is perhaps therefore no surprise that they threw themselves enthusiastically into the task of manufacturing a replacement source of identity. Without a group as a reference point, it can be hard to know who you are.

Minimal groups

Sherif believed that it was the conflict of interests between groups which led to intergroup hostility. But this view came to be challenged in the 1970s and 1980s, culminating in the development of social identity theory by Henri Tajfel (Tajfel and Turner, 1979; Abrams and Hogg, 1990). As mentioned in Chapter 1, Tajfel's social psychology was European rather than North American in origin, and he was keen to encourage a less individualistic flavour to the discipline. It is therefore no surprise that his focus of interest was in the group as a source of social identity. During the late-1960s and 1970s, Tajfel had been investigating the origins of intergroup conflict by the use of an experimental paradigm known as the 'minimal group'. Experiments using this paradigm appear to show that simply knowing that one has been assigned to a group, where the group has no identifiable characteristics and where one never gets to meet other group members, is sufficient for members to exercise favouritism for other group members and discrimination against out-group members. In Tajfel's original experiment (Tajfel *et al.*, 1971) experimental groups were created using English schoolboys. They were each individually tested on a task which asked them to estimate the number of dots projected briefly on to a screen. Depending on their responses, they were told that they were either 'underestimators' or 'overestimators'. They were then told (deceived) that another researcher was conducting an experiment on rewards and penalties, and wanted to use the two groups. Again, the boys took part in the experiment individually. There had been no opportunity for a group culture or interpersonal relationships to develop between members of the groups and the task they were given did not involve straightforward conflict of interests, although it provided opportunities for favouritism and discrimination to emerge.

The task involved the presentation of a number of payoff matrices, where the boys were required to choose one from a number of pairs of points that could be awarded to two other boys, who were identified only by a number and by whether they were an underestimator or an overestimator. The total number of points awarded to each boy at the end of the experiment was translated into a monetary reward. The possible choices allowed the boys to opt for different strategies: maximising the in-group's profits, maximising both groups' profits, maximising the difference between their profits, or giving equal profits to both groups. Tajfel found that the boys opted for a middle-of-the-road strategy, where modest profits were allocated to each group but where the in-group always received slightly more. They seemed to be opting for the fairest solution that still allowed them to give their own group the edge. Brown (1988a) provides a real-life parallel to the minimal group findings in disputes over wage differentials, where workers are less concerned about the absolute wage levels in their own and other occupations but are more anxious to preserve an appropriate difference between these to signal the greater status of their own occupation.

A number of similar studies have since produced results supporting Tajfel's findings, and although a variety of artefactual explanations have been offered, it seems likely that there is a real group phenomenon operating here (Brown, 1988a; Augoustinos and Walker, 1995). These results are startling because the groups were indeed minimal: they could be said to exist only in the minds of the boys. There was no history of interaction between group members or between groups, no shared culture or norms – nothing to link the members together except for their identification as an underestimator or an overestimator. In order to account for the findings, Tajfel developed social identity theory.

Social identity theory

Tajfel argued that the reason why we are so ready to take on board the position of group member, no matter how fleeting or tenuous, and to favour our in-group above the out-group is that group membership is vital to our self-esteem. To the extent that our sense of self, our identity, is derived from the groups we belong to, we can only feel good about ourselves if we can maximise the status, prestige and success of the groups we identify with. Social identity theory involves three fundamental processes. These are

85

categorisation, identity and comparison. Tajfel argues that categorisation is a basic human capacity, an aspect of human nature. We are predisposed to order and structure our perceptions of the world (including the social world) into categories. We divide up the world according to a multitude of dichotomies such as animate–inanimate, rural–urban, masculine–feminine and us–them. We are then able to locate ourselves as members of some categories and not others. Although the categories we use to structure our world are invented by human beings (rather than being intrinsic to the natural world itself) of course each person or generation does not make up its own categories: we inherit them from previous generations through our culture. These categories are therefore social and shared. In order for the categories that we use to be functional for us, it is important that we can clearly distinguish between class and non-class members. For example, if you park your car in a no-parking zone, you will need to be able to quickly and efficiently tell the difference between a traffic warden and other members of the public. Tajfel therefore argues that we are also predisposed to *accentuate* in our perception the similarities between members of a category and the differences between members of different categories, so that the distinctions between class and non-class members are very sharp. Thus, we come to see ourselves as more similar to members of our own categories and different from members of other categories, and the process of accentuation explains why we tend to stereotype people whom we identify as belonging to a particular group.

Once we locate ourselves as members of certain groups or categories, our identity is derived from these. When we answer the question 'Who am I?' with answers such as 'I am a student', 'I am a citizen of the USA', 'I am a Muslim' and 'I am a teenager', we are constructing our identity from our membership of these groups. So our identity is a combination of all the many group memberships we hold. Of course not all of these are salient for us at any one time, and different situations will call forth different aspects of our identity as our different group affiliations become relevant or irrelevant. For example, you may be having a conversation with some acquaintances when someone remarks that higher education is a waste of money. Your identity as student would then become salient to the interaction, and you may suddenly become aware of yourself *as a student*, whereas this aspect of your identity had previously been in the background. I remember an occasion when, as an undergraduate, I was enjoying a social gathering in a pub with a boyfriend and a large group of friends from his course. I knew and liked each of them as individuals, and I had not been consciously aware of the fact that I was the only women in the group until one of the men, who had been about to tell a rather 'blue' joke said 'Oh, I'd better save it for later – there's a lady present'. At this point my identity as female suddenly became salient and thrown into sharp relief for me. I then was posed with the question of how to continue with the interaction 'as a woman'. This example shows how, through the interactional gambits of others, we may find ourselves the bearers of identities that we had not sought for ourselves, but that nevertheless we must deal with in some way. Some group identities only come into being occasionally and transiently, for example in a queue, where we feel a common ground with others who are unreasonably kept waiting, but others are salient for us in many of our relations, like our membership of gender and nationality categories, occupational or religious groups and so on, and form major aspects of our identity. Others, such as football fan, may be episodic, called forth primarily on Saturday afternoons. Or they may occupy a central place in our identity, as in the case of the main character of the book (later made into a film) *Fever pitch*, an Arsenal football club supporter for whom the ebb and flow of his personal fortunes and self-esteem is almost entirely determined by the successes and failures of the team.

It is vital to our self-esteem that the identity we are able to construct for ourselves is a positive and valued one. We are therefore predisposed to think highly of the groups and categories to which we are affiliated. If being Irish is generally seen to be a good thing, then our own status as an Irish person has an enhancing effect on our identity and our self-esteem. The esteem-value of group membership is beautifully illustrated in Groucho Marx's famous comedic line, 'Please accept my resignation. I don't want to belong to any club that will accept me as a member'. Of course, we cannot always choose the groups to which we belong, for example our gender and ethnicity, and may take pains to distance ourselves from categories that threaten to reduce our self-esteem. But just recognising that one is a member of particular groups is not sufficient to guarantee self-esteem. The high value placed on membership of some categories only has significance when compared to the lesser value attached to other groups. It is therefore the *comparisons* that we make between the qualities of our own group and those of the out-group that provide the basis for our self-esteem, with the consequent tendency to valorise our own group and derogate the qualities and members of comparison groups. The 'Rattlers' and 'Eagles' in Sherif's study were doing just this, and in terms of social identity theory they were motivated by the need to establish positive identities for themselves that would furnish them with a good measure of self-esteem.

The minimal group experiments and social identity theory were devised to explain intergroup conflict, and there has been considerable debate concerning the extent to which conflict in the real world can be understood in these terms. Nevertheless, regardless of its relevance to this issue, the theory itself has much to offer for our understanding of identity. It is one of the few theories emerging from psychological social psychology to postulate a thoroughly social understanding of the person and to regard the social realm as more than a set of variables which may come to influence the ready-made person.

Reference groups

Psychological social psychology's interest in groups has been exclusively focused upon the groups, real or experimental, to which people can be said to belong. Although it takes a much more social stance than most social psychology, social identity theory likewise focuses upon the potential for identity formation present in the actual groups and categories that a person belongs to. But a person's identity may only be partially defined by these.

We may try to distance ourselves from our membership of groups that offer us only damaging identities, and likewise may identify with groups to which we do not, or even could not, aspire. Hyman (1942) introduced the concept of the 'reference group' to refer to such groups, and it is a concept that has been taken up primarily by sociological social psychologists, particularly symbolic interactionists. A reference group may be defined as 'any group, formal, informal or symbolic, in which the individual has a psychologically functioning membership' (Newcombe, 1951). Likewise, Shibutani (1955) argues that the power of the concept lies in its capacity to explain behaviour that is directed toward audiences that are not obviously present, audiences that may represent groups to whom the actor does not belong. For example, Shibutani cites a study of members of a trades union by Goldstein (1959), who found that engineers in a factory, in contrast to the industrial workers, took on a typically middle-class perspective in their opposition to industrial action. The comic character and 'telephone voice' of the working-class woman who aspires to a middle-class identity is another example, as is the inverted snobbery of her middle-class counterpart serving steak and kidney pudding to her dinner guests.

The reference group also gives us some purchase on lifestyle choices as they are evidenced in dress, musical taste and décor. In the UK, the oak-beamed 'farmhouse' kitchen and the Regency-style dining room speak of the different reference groups of the people inhabiting them. They 'refer to' the presumed values and lifestyles of previous eras. It might be argued that reference groups (as opposed to the actual groups to which we may belong) are coming to play a more and more central role in our identity construction, at least in Western, industrialised societies. The geographical and social mobility that is the hallmark of such societies means that people are less likely than formerly to be fully present in the kinship and community networks where they grew up. People change their jobs and even their careers much more frequently than did earlier generations, so that occupational as well as family roles may offer only temporary and weak opportunities for our identities to crystallise around these.

But Shibutani, drawing on symbolic interactionism, further distinguishes between the *people* who make up an audience and the *perspective* that is imputed to an audience. He emphasises that Mead's concept of the generalised other does not refer to actual other people but to a shared perspective. He sees a reference group as 'that group whose presumed perspective is used by an actor as the frame of reference in the organisation of his perceptual field . . . a reference group is an audience, consisting of real or imaginary personifications, to whom certain values are imputed' (p. 132). In talking of perspectives rather than real audiences, Shibutani makes the reference group into something much more pervasive than a real group – rather than a reference *group* it becomes a *frame* of reference, a system of unquestioned assumptions and beliefs that structure a person's perception of the world, and to the extent that this perception is shared by others a person may be said to be a part of the same society: 'Each socialized person, then, is a society in miniature. Once he has incorporated the culture of his group, it becomes his perspective, and he can bring this frame of reference to bear upon all new situations that he encounters' (p. 132). Whatever their cultural origin, people who share a culture, by definition, share a set of assumptions that are 'ground' rather than 'figure' for them. Such assumptions are therefore rarely articulated or consciously stated, and it is only when a member of that culture contravenes or challenges one of these assumptions that we become aware that there *is* an assumption at all. For example, the norms governing social interaction are invisible until someone breaks a rule by standing too close in conversation or addressing you in too familiar or too formal way for the occasion. Making visible the invisible assumptions held by members of a society was at the heart of the methodology adopted by Howard Garfinkel in the 1960s in a series of what he called 'breaching experiments'. He instructed his students to engage in some unusual behaviours in public, for example singing loudly while on a bus or haggling over the price of goods in a shop, and to observe people's reactions. This is why we can consider each person a society in miniature, and why the dualism between the individual and society is misleading.

Individuals carry around with them the unwritten assumptions of their society, and routinely practise them in the course of their daily interactions with other members of that society. Each individual is in this sense a small-scale copy of their society.

The reference group as a 'frame of reference', then, may constitute the entire society or culture that we belong to. It is all those others whose perspective we are sharing or assuming when we speak and act. Mead used the term 'the generalised other' to refer to this shared perspective, and it has an important part to play in the development of the self. Mead's view shares with a number of other perspectives the basic idea that the self is of social origin, but it differs from them in the extent to which the person is seen as *determined* by social forces. The extent to which the person is conceived as having agency in the development of their selfhood is discussed below.

The social origins of the self

The generalised other

As we saw in Chapter 3, Mead saw 'taking the role of the other' as the process by which we are able to come to have a self-concept. We experience ourselves only indirectly; we become objects to ourselves, gaining some concept of how we appear to others, as we take the role of the other during social interaction. So our reflections on how we appear to specific others in our social environment contributes to the development of our self-concept. But our social encounters do not just consist of interactions in dyads (pairs). We take part in social situations where there may be numerous other participants, and Mead claims that as we grow up we become able to conceive of ourselves as viewed from the perspective of people in general – the generalised other. The generalised other, then, gives us a composite self-concept that does not depend upon our interactions with specific others, and which is inevitably imbued with the shared assumptions of our social group. The significance of the generalised other for our self-concept does not just lie in the information it provides concerning oneself as one is reflected in the eyes of others. Taking the role of the generalised other means that, as well as seeing ourselves through the eyes of others, we are also able to see interactions between others from this general vantage point, and to take on the perspective of the generalised other in our view of the activities and endeavours that our society or culture is engaged upon. We therefore come to fully share in our society's taken-for-granted assumptions and they become just as much a part of our self-concept as other components that are acquired through taking the role of specific others: 'only in so far as he takes the attitudes of the organized social group to which he belongs toward the organized, co-operative social activity or set of such activities in which that group as such is engaged, does he develop a complete self . . .' (Mead, 1956, p. 106). When we express a view or take a stance, we are very often expressing the perspective of the gener-alised other:

> If we say 'This is my property, I shall control it,' that affir-mation calls out a certain set of responses which must be the same in any community in which property exists. It involves an organized attitude with reference to property which is common to all the members of the community. One must have a definite attitude of control of his own property and respect for the property of others. Those atti-tudes (as organized sets of responses) must be there on the part of all, so that when one says such a thing he calls out in himself the response of the others. He is calling out the response of what I have called a generalized other.
>
> (Mead, 1956, p. 110)

Mead viewed such attitudes as just as much a part of the person's personality as anything that is unique to him or her (if such uniqueness is possible). As psychologists, we have a tendency to only regard as aspects of the personality those features that *distinguish* a person from others, and to view our personality as that which exists over and above socially shared attitudes and characteristics, a view engendered by the individualism and dualism at the heart of the discipline. In Mead's view, the tacit assumptions that we share as members of a society are just as much a part of our personalities as anything that marks us out as different.

Nevertheless, Blumer (1962) (who introduced the term 'symbolic interactionism') argues that, unlike many sociologists, Mead did not conceive of the person as simply a product of social forces. Such a view would be deterministic in just the same way that many psychological theories are. The defining feature of mind for Mead is the reflectiveness that taking the role of the other entails. We are able to anticipate the meaning that our behaviour will hold for others and to choose our course of action accordingly. This ability to choose means that we are not simply socially (or psychologically) determined. For Mead, the self refers to this cycle of reflectiveness and choice, which has two components. The self proper refers to the part of the cycle where the person reflects their own actions and potential actions as seen through the eyes of others. The self-concept is the outcome of these reflections, the composite picture of us that we build up by seeing ourselves from the vantage point of others. Mead used the terms 'I' and 'Me' to refer to these two aspects of self. Nevertheless, as Ashworth (1979) points out, even this reflectiveness, this choice, is socially derived. This is because our deliberations and reflections (mind) are themselves internalised social interactions, dialogues with others carried out privately, the legacy of our emergence as a self through taking-the-role-of-the-other during social interaction (see Chapter 3). Thus, for Mead, the self is thoroughly social in origin.

The 'looking-glass' self

Some of the flavour of Mead's account can be seen in earlier theoretical formulations. Charles Horton Cooley was a contemporary of Mead and was professor of sociology at the University of Michigan. In 1902 he published *Human nature and the social order*, and the ideas he presented there were taken up in some measure in the development of symbolic interactionism. One of the key ideas in this book is the 'looking-glass self'. Here, Cooley argues that the thoughts and behaviours that we ordinarily think of as uncomplicatedly emanating from and belonging to 'me' are always implicitly thought or enacted with reference to others: 'Thus, if we think of a secluded part of the woods as "ours", it is because we think, also, that others do not go there' (p. 181) and 'There is no sense of "I", as in pride or shame, without its correlative sense of you, or he, or they' (p. 182). The 'looking-glass self' describes how our self-concept is derived from our relations with others. Cooley claims that we imagine how we appear to others, then further imagine what the others' judgement of us is, and then respond accordingly:

> As we see our face, figure and dress in the glass, and are interested in them because they are ours, and pleased or otherwise with them according as they do or do not answer to what we should like them to be; so in imagination we perceive in another's mind some thought of our appearance, manners, aims, deeds, character, friends, and so on, and are variously affected by it . . . We always imagine, and in imagining share, the judgements of the other mind.
>
> (pp. 184–185)

Although he does not explicitly state this, Cooley appears to suggest that we have no choice but to internalise others' views of us. The self we develop would then be nothing more than a picture built up of ourselves as reflected in and appraised through the eyes of others. We can see the similarity between this and Mead's 'taking-the-role-of-the-other', but Mead goes beyond the idea of the looking-glass self in his account of the reflective process (the 'I'), that gives us some control over who we are and what we do. Ashworth (2000) suggests that this reflective process allows for the possibility of the development of a relatively autonomous self-concept, so that instead of our assessment of our potential actions always being limited to how they may be seen in the eyes of others, we can evaluate them against our own self-concept. This analysis permits the self to escape from the tyranny of other-determination.

The self-fulfilling prophecy

The power of others' perceptions to shape who we are has been recognised by psychologists and sociologists alike. A variety of terms have been used to describe and explain this phenomenon, such as 'expectations', 'stereotyping', 'self-fulfilling prophecy' and 'labelling'. There is a considerable body of research evidence supporting the claim that people come to acquire characteristics and identities that are attributed to them by others, although the mechanisms by which this is supposed to occur are not always fully explained theoretically.

The sociologist Robert Merton based his idea of the self-fulfilling prophecy on Thomas's concept of the definition of the situation (see pp. 26–7, Chapter 2). Quoting Thomas's view that 'If men define situations as real, they are real in their consequences', Merton (1948) applies it to a specific example. In 1932, The Last National Bank went out of business on what was afterwards known as 'Black Wednesday', due to the spread of a (false) rumour that the bank was insolvent. As the rumour spread, more and more of the bank's depositors rushed to withdraw their money, and the bank indeed became insolvent. Once the bank's situation came to be defined as insolvent, this definition had real consequences. Merton goes on to argue that the same process can be used to explain important social problems of the day, such as racial prejudice. He gives the example of the stereotype of 'Negroes' (the usual term employed at that time) as strike breakers, who were typically characterised as having a low standard of living and prepared to take white men's jobs by working for lower pay. On the basis of their apparent lack of respect for working-class solidarity, they were excluded from trades unions. Merton argues that this (false) definition of the situation led to a situation in which, out of work following the First World War and excluded from the trades unions, these men had little choice but to agree to work for strikebound employers, and thus indeed became 'scabs'. The stereotype, as a definition of the situation, became a reality, a self-fulfilling prophecy.

Rosenthal and Jacobson (1968a) drew on the notion of the self-fulfilling prophecy in their famous study of the effects of teachers' expectations on educational performance, which was later published as the book, *Pygmalion in the classroom* (Rosenthal and Jacobson, 1968b). They were concerned with the under-performance of some children in North American schools. As in Britain, these children were likely to be poor, and to be from ethnic minority groups. They were seen as disadvantaged, and this term also serves as an explanation since such children are often perceived as suffering a lack of educational resources and encouragement at home. But Rosenthal and Jacobson questioned this causal connection and argued that it is teachers who set up low expectations for these children because of their own perceptions of their background as disadvantaged. In a field study, they used an elementary school in San Francisco with a predominantly lower-class catchment, including families on welfare and Mexican-Americans, and randomly selected about five children from each class. The teachers were told (deceived) that these children had been identified as 'intellectual spurters' by a new intelligence test that had been given to all the children at the end of the previous school year. They were told that the children identified could be expected to make greater than average intellectual gains in the next academic year. Several months later, IQ tests showed that those children had indeed made greater gains than the rest. The teachers also perceived these children as happier, more curious, appealing and better adjusted, and needing less social approval.

It seemed unlikely that these gains could be explained by the teachers spending more time with these children. When asked, the teachers did not report any such differences but, more convincingly, in any given class the more the spurters gained, the greater the gains showed by the rest of the children in the class. The researchers suggested instead that the process is more subtle, that the teachers' expectations were communicated by their tone of voice, facial expression, touch and posture. They discuss the possibility that the results could be due to the Hawthorne effect, where participants who are singled out for attention or intervention in a study make gains in performance simply because of the morale-boosting effects of being the focus of attention. Nevertheless, even if this were so, the teachers' and children's perceptions of the latter's 'specialness' as the active ingredient in the change would still locate educational performance as open to social influence rather than being simply the outcome of relatively stable cognitive abilities.

But what exactly is it that is happening to these students to induce such a change? Evidence cited by Salmon (1998) suggests that the self-concept or identity of the child is influential in educational performance. She quotes a study by Hartley (1986), using 7–8-year-old disadvantaged children who had been judged to be of low ability by their teachers. He gave them the Matching Familiar Figures Test, which involves matching a figure with an identical one when it is placed in a series of slightly different figures. Responses on this test are marked in terms of 'impulsiveness' versus 'reflectiveness', where impulsiveness is statistically related to low intelligence. Hartley administered the test, and then asked the children to do it again, but this time while imagining that they are someone who is very clever. Hartley found that when doing the task 'as themselves', the children performed impulsively, making many errors, but when acting as 'someone clever' they were much more cautious and concerned with accuracy and their scores showed more reflectiveness. Salmon concludes:

> For traditional ways of thinking about competence, this outcome seems almost incomprehensible. We generally suppose individual differences in ability to be an innate property of people, as fixed and unalterable as the colour of our eyes. Yet children, in playfully exchanging personal identities, can, apparently at will, perform at levels of competence assumed to be beyond them. This can only mean that what we call intellectual ability, so far from being an inborn set of limits, is at least in part a product of the kinds of people we are, or are seen to be.
>
> (p. 66)

It may therefore be that the teachers in Rosenthal and Jacobson's study were subtly providing the spurters with a revised identity or self-concept, an identity consistent with a higher level of academic performance. Nevertheless, their findings were not straightforward. For example, children who showed an unexpected gain in IQ were rated less favourably by their teachers, especially for children in low-ability groups. Even when their gain was expected, their teachers tended to view such children unfavourably in terms of adjustment and future success. People whose behaviour seems to contradict our stereotypical expectations of them may therefore go down in our estimation rather than succeed in changing our stereotypes.

Using a laboratory experiment, Snyder et al. (1977) demonstrated that stereotypes, although they may actually have little or no truth in them, if they are believed can lead to changes in the way we behave toward people. In communicating our expectations through our interaction with them, we can encourage those people to adopt the expected characteristics. Snyder et al. use the 'what is beautiful is good' stereotype. This is the tendency of people to attribute other positive qualities to those who are seen as attractive. Male 'perceivers' interacted via an audio connection with female 'targets' whom they believed to be physically attractive or unattractive. In fact, they were provided with a photograph of one of a number of women previously rated by other males as either very attractive or very unattractive and (falsely) believed this to be the woman with whom they were interacting. The interaction was tape-recorded and the interaction style of the participants was judged by naïve observers. The results showed that the women who were believed to be attractive were perceived by the men as more friendly and sociable, and indeed behaved in a more friendly, likeable and sociable manner. The men were observed to behave differently with 'attractive' women, with whom they were warm, sociable, humorous and outgoing. These findings appear to support Rosenthal and Jacobson's hypothesis that expectations are communicated through the quality of interpersonal interaction.

In their discussion, Snyder et al. remark that 'Social observers have for decades commented on the ways in which stigmatised social groups and outsiders may fall "victim" to self-fulfilling cultural stereotypes' (p. 53) and cite symbolic interactionist writers such as Howard Becker and Erving Goffman, both of whom had written about the powerful social expectations shaping the lives and identities of people who are in some way seen as deviant or marginal to society. These writers lead us into a consideration of labelling as a form of widespread stereotyping operating at the social level. Stereotyping tends to be thought of as a psychological concept – we think of stereotypes as something akin to attitudes or opinions that are the property of individual minds. But labels carry a different connotation. Labels are conferred upon things by people. Just as we may label a jar 'coffee' because of what is inside it (and *expected* to be inside it) we confer labels upon other people, which must then be borne by them.

Labelling

Labelling is the social counterpart to stereotyping, but, as Ashworth (1979) points out, the concept of stereotyping does not necessarily imply that the stereotyped person will come to adopt the characteristics of the stereotype or be materially affected in some other way by it. The concept of labelling explicitly focuses upon the consequences of the label for the person labelled.

Becker (1963) developed labelling theory as a result of his research and writing on deviance, and the theory is generally located within the framework of symbolic interactionism since it places importance upon the role of social interaction and the negotiation of the meaning of events. Unlike most theorists at the time, Becker was not interested in explaining deviance in terms of personality characteristics or upbringing. Instead he was concerned firstly with how certain behaviours and characteristics become seen as deviant by a social group and secondly with how the label of 'deviant' is then applied, accepted or resisted. Thus, labelling is a process of conflict, bargaining and negotiation: '*Social groups create deviance by making rules whose infraction constitutes deviance*, and by applying these rules to particular people and labelling them as outsiders ... The deviant is one to whom that label has successfully been applied; deviant behaviour is behaviour that people so label' (Becker, 1963, p. 9, italics in original).

But labelling is also a process suffused by power relations.

Some persons or groups are able to impose their rules on others, which Becker (1963) called 'moral entrepreneurship'. Becker recognised that political and economic power is influential in deciding who is defined as deviant and on what grounds. Many people commit acts that might be seen as deviant but not all get labelled as such. However, it is more likely that your acts will be labelled 'deviant' if you are working-class, poor or black. Young people involved in a fight in a low-income neighbourhood are likely to be seen by police as delinquent, but in a wealthy neighbourhood their behaviour would be regarded as just 'youthful high spirits'. Powerful groups, such as the police, courts, doctors, media etc. are influential in making sure that the identity sticks. Becker (1963) reports that boys from middle-class areas, when compared with boys from slum areas, are less likely to be taken to the police station if they are picked up, less likely to be charged/booked and are very unlikely to be convicted and sentenced. However, Becker may be criticised for seeming to adopt too deterministic a view and for ignoring the role of the labelled individual in creating or resisting their deviant identity. If an individual is labelled deviant in some way, that identity tends to be a powerful influence in all social interactions where others are aware of the label so that there are pressures on the labelled person to accept the identity. But there are also resources for resisting it. For example, gay persons can turn to their community for supportive alternative self-definitions, and juvenile delinquents may turn to each other to redefine and justify their behaviour.

Nevertheless, labels may become part of the person's identity through a process of re-defining their own behaviour. Once offered to us, labels become a kind of filter through which we see our behaviour, both past and present, and we begin to see it in a new light. The boy who has successive run-ins with police (through bad luck) and is called a juvenile delinquent may begin to think of himself differently. He may seek out other similar delinquents for support, strengthening his affiliation with deviant sub-cultures, with the consequence that he may go on to commit further acts that are seen by him as consistent with and deriving from the new identity. The original (primary) deviant act may not have been seen as such, but gets redefined in retrospect. 'Mentally ill' is another good example. Everyone has times when their behaviour may be thought a little odd, but if you are labelled 'mentally ill' it is more likely that you will come to see such episodes as evidence of mental illness. Furthermore, Scheff (1969) argues that those who have been labelled as deviant are often rewarded for accepting the label. For example, mental patients who show insight into their condition (that is, accept that they are mentally ill and see their past behaviour as evidence of their illness) are rewarded by psychiatrists and other hospital staff. Individuals who try to adopt a more conventional identity in the future (after release from hospital) often face an uphill struggle to leave behind their former identity and forge conventional work, family and community roles.

In a remarkable and famous study by Rosenhan (1973), the researcher and seven other sane people contrived to get themselves admitted to various mental hospitals by claiming that they heard voices. After being admitted, they were instructed to get themselves discharged as quickly as possible by behaving in a normal and sane manner. However, their sanity was not recognised by the hospital staff, and each of them was eventually discharged (after an average stay of 19 days) with a diagnosis of 'schizophrenia in remission'. In fact, there was a considerable tendency among the staff for the behaviour and personal biographies of the 'patients' to be construed as confirming the diagnosis. For example, the pseudo-patients were asked to take daily notes on their experiences. Note-taking was never challenged by staff, but for one pseudo-patient it was often recorded in nurses' records as 'patient engages in writing behaviour'. Rosenhan argues that staff assumed that, since the person was in a mental hospital he must be disturbed and therefore his behaviour must be a manifestation of his disturbance. In addition, interactions between pseudo-patients and staff had a particular character. Pseudo-patients had been instructed to regularly approach appropriate members of staff with reasonable requests for information, such as 'Pardon me, Dr X. Could you tell me when I am eligible for grounds privileges?' Rosenhan reports that staff typically responded to such questions either with a minimal answer as they passed on their way, averting their gaze, or by ignoring them altogether. This is an example of a more pervasive 'depersonalization' experienced by patients and pseudo-patients, some of which amounted to acts of maltreatment and cruelty.

The label 'mentally ill' therefore has powerful effects upon the definition of people's behaviour, both in terms of other's perceptions of them and in terms of their self-perceptions. Labelling is a similar idea to the self-fulfilling prophecy discussed above, but in addition it provides a useful analysis of the processes by which labels may come to have a real influence upon the person's self-concept and behaviour as well as their social identity.

Summary

Studies of intergroup conflict and the findings of minimal group research suggest that groups are an important source of our identity; they give us a sense of who we are. In his social identity theory, Tajfel further suggests that our group memberships also provide us with potential sources of self-esteem. What is illustrated here is the extensive role of social groups in the shaping of our personhood. Unlike most psychological social psychologists, Tajfel seems to see groups as producing (rather than simply influencing) who we are. Social identity theory does not appear to posit the existence of a pre-social individual, although the theory does not explicitly address this issue and is undeniably cognitive and therefore psychological rather than sociological in flavour. But the view that our membership of groups and cultures may provide the basis for much, if not all, of our sense of self is developed further by symbolic interactionism. Both Cooley and Mead took the view that our sense of self is derived from our ability to see ourselves through other's eyes in our interactions with each other. But Mead's account additionally gives the person the power to reflect upon such perceptions and to have a hand in the development of our own self-concept, enabling us to be more than simply the unwitting products of others' perceptions.

Labelling theory, which was derived from the fundamental assumptions of symbolic interactionism, and the concept of the self-fulfilling prophecy are both accounts of how our identities are socially bestowed, negotiated and maintained, and labelling theory additionally provides some insight into how social identities may become part of our self-concept. In broad terms, therefore, social identity theory, symbolic interactionism, the self-fulfilling prophecy and labelling are not inconsistent with each other, but symbolic interactionist theory additionally spells out how the social 'gets inside' the person.

Symbolic interactionism is not the only social psychology to give a central role to social processes in the explanation of our identity and sense of self. In the next chapter, I will examine more recent formulations emerging within psychology that, each in its own way and to a greater or lesser extent, makes the person contingent upon social processes.

Suggested further reading

Augoustinos, M. and Walker, I. (1995) *Social cognition: an integrated introduction*. London: Sage.
Brown, R. (1988) *Group processes: dynamics within and between groups*. Oxford: Blackwell.

Chapter 5

Representations
and language

IN THE PREVIOUS TWO CHAPTERS, I have
looked at the importance of social roles, relationships and groups in understanding one's
identity and sense of self. The argument at the
heart of both of these chapters was that 'who
I am' is socially produced, a socially bestowed,
negotiated and maintained phenomenon, and the
focus has been upon the crucial part played
by other people in our identity formation. In the
present chapter I shall be continuing with the
theme of the social construction of self and
identity, but the focus is here upon the role of
representations and language. This focus upon
language is characteristic of more recent developments in social psychology that have been
influenced by European social psychology and
social theory. The reader may notice that some of
the arguments put forward here bear more than a
passing resemblance to symbolic interactionism,

which also puts language centre-stage. Although there are similarities, the theoretical positions discussed in this chapter have not
primarily been derived from symbolic interactionism, having their
roots in European philosophical and theoretical traditions that
have led parallel lives to the symbolic interactionism of North
America. Where appropriate, I will comment upon the extent to
which these theories can be seen as sharing common assumptions.

Social representations

In Chapter 4, through the exploration of concepts such as reference groups and the generalised other, we saw how individuals
are thought to assume the common-sense beliefs and ways of
thinking prevalent in their society. Moscovici (1984) described
these taken-for-granted assumptions as social representations.
These shared assumptions about the nature of the world and of
human beings, it is argued, enable people in a society to make
sense of their experience, to communicate effectively with each
other and to co-ordinate their activities. To take the example
quoted by Mead in Chapter 4, to the extent that people in a
society all implicitly believe in the ownership of personal property, this gives rise to a whole array of shared social practices
including fitting locks on your doors and taking out insurance
policies, the development of property laws, policing activities,
giving gifts and teaching your children to share. Even the use of
money itself would make little sense if there were no such thing
as personal property. None of these things would be widespread
social practices and some of them would not even be possible
(such as insurance, which depends upon large numbers of people
making the same assumptions) if individual people all practised
different beliefs regarding property. Social representations may
therefore be characteristic of whole societies. But of course not
everyone in a society holds exactly the same beliefs on everything,
so that sub-cultures and groups have their own characteristic
social representations of some things. For example, the British
National Front and the Ku Klux Klan in America are charac-

terised by representations of race not shared to the same extent by the rest of their respective societies. The Hippie movement of the 1960s was characterised by representations of love and sexuality and by a work ethic that conflicted with the assumptions fundamental to the commonly accepted North American way of life at the time. For Moscovici, it is these shared social representations that gives a group its groupness; where there are shared social representations, we can say that a group, rather than just an ad hoc collection of people, exists.

G.W. Allport (1954), the younger brother of F.H. Allport (see Chapter 1) shared his brother's emphasis on the individual and had cited Auguste Comte as the ancestor of his vision of social psychology, firmly locating it as a positivistic science, but Moscovici cites the French sociologist Emile Durkheim as his influence. He based the concept of social representations on Durkheim's (1898) notion of 'collective representations'. Collective representations are the myths, legends and belief systems that characterise a society, and Durkheim felt that these just could not be properly understood at the level of the individual; they are truly social phenomena. Like Durkheim, Moscovici felt strongly that the study of these was the proper business of social psychology, and that the discipline's preoccupation with a positivistic science of the individual had led down a blind alley. He says, in characteristic Gallic style: 'Despite numerous further studies, fragmentary ideas and experiments, we are now no more advanced than we were nearly a century ago. Our knowledge is like a mayonnaise which has curdled' (Moscovici, 1984, p. 13).

Moscovici preferred the term 'social representations' for his own theory because Durkheim's idea appeared rather static and deterministic. It seemed to suggest that people's thinking is determined and limited by their collective representations and that these are relatively stable over time. Moscovici wanted to keep Durkheim's focus on the shared and consensual nature of representations. Like the myths and belief systems of traditional societies, they are our common sense, our society's unquestioned assumptions about the world. But he also wanted to emphasise how they are continually shaped and re-shaped by people during social interaction. Social representations are therefore neither straitjackets forced onto us by society nor the original products of individuals' thinking. Although they may pre-exist our birth into a particular society, they are plastic, malleable and subject to re-formulation through their everyday appropriation and use by individuals in their dealings with each other. But at the same time, social representations powerfully shape our perceptions of and thinking about the world; it is social representations and not objective properties of the world that provide our perception of it. For example, Moscovici takes issue with the claims made by attribution theory. Attribution theories argue that people make decisions about the causes of events or of others' behaviour based on the cognitive processing of available information (see Chapter 6). A basic attribution decision concerns whether we see an event as caused by something external to the person or by dispositional (internal) factors. But Moscovici argues that we don't assign a cause to an event on the grounds of the evidence; rather, we select the evidence according to the factors we already believe to cause events of that kind (the representation we have adopted). Situational and dispositional attributions are not alternative outcomes of information processing but political standpoints identified with particular social representations. It is therefore no surprise that, for example, tendencies to adopt the 'just world' view (that people get what they deserve) has been found to be characteristic of privileged classes and not a feature of human nature in general.

All human interactions presuppose these representations since any interaction must be based on shared meanings or a definition of the situation, but they are also *created* by people in interaction. Nevertheless, once created, a representation leads a seemingly autonomous life, merging with other representations, swallowing up old ones, and giving birth to new ones. Therefore, although social representations are seen as operating at the level of society, nevertheless they are also manifested and may be studied at the level of the individual person. Because of its phenomenological flavour and its emphasis upon the central role of social interaction, Deutscher (1984) claims that the theory of social representations owes more to symbolic interactionism, North American pragmatism and phenomenology than the structural-functionalism of Durkheim. In fact Moscovici (1984) explicitly refers to Mead, agreeing with him that we conduct ourselves according to the meaning that events have for us, and that this meaning issues at least in part from our common language, common values and common experiences as members of the same society or group.

Because he sees social representations as existing at, and therefore available for study at, the individual as well as the social level, Moscovici goes into some detail about the psychological processes he believes underlie their transmission and transformation. In this sense the theory of social representations is a genuine attempt to bridge the gap between sociological and psychological social psychologies. Just as Mead used concepts such as taking the role of the other and the 'I' and the 'Me' to explain how the social gets inside people, Moscovici developed his own theoretical concepts for explaining how social representations become part of a person's psychology, while at the same time becoming changed and recycled. This part of the theory is explicitly cognitive in nature, focusing upon mental processes such as thought, imagination and memory. Representations have both conceptual and pictorial elements: the abstract concepts and images that embody the idea.

Moscovici sees fear of the unknown and the unfamiliar as a basic human characteristic. We all need to make sense of our experience, to give it a shape and a name. Representations serve an important psychological function: they render the unfamiliar familiar. When we try to make sense of something new and unfamiliar, we search among our memories and past experiences for something that resembles it until we can identify it, with relief, as 'one of those'. This recognition is important because it gives us some purchase on our experience and enables us to formulate some kind of appropriate response. Without some notion of 'what has just happened' we would be behaviourally paralysed (as indeed sometimes happens when we are initially unable to take in some event). This moment of classification and naming is termed 'anchoring'. We are able to anchor unfamiliar things in this way by comparing the new event or object with prototype cases from different classes of events in our experience. Prototypes are models or typical examples of a class of events, and consist of a set of salient features:

> The main virtue of a class, that which makes it so easy to handle, is that it provides a suitable model or prototype to represent the class and a sort of photo-kit of all the individuals supposed to belong to it. This photo-kit represents a sort of test case that sums up the features common to a number of related cases, that is, on the one hand, an idealised conflation of salient points and, on the other, an iconic matrix of readily identifiable points. Thus, most of us, as our visual representation of a Frenchman, have an image of an undersized person wearing a beret and carrying a long loaf of French bread.
>
> (1984, p. 31)

Moscovici therefore shares Tajfel's view (see Chapter 4) that categorisation is a fundamental feature of human psychology. We look for the things that may mark out someone, something or some event as a member of a category. He quotes a study by Denise Jodelet of French villagers' reactions to mental patients who came to live in their community. The nearest categories already available to the villagers in order to understand the unfamiliar behaviour of their new neighbours were 'idiots', 'tramps' and 'rogues', and the mental patients came to be seen by them in terms of these representations. But once an event or object becomes anchored to a representation, it is then readily seen as possessing its typical characteristic features. Jodelet's villagers noticed the behavioural oddities of the mental patients more readily than their general hard-working and pleasant nature.

A second process, called 'objectification', further adds to this familiarisation of the unfamiliar and gives representations their characteristic and reassuring feeling of solidity. For example, when people talk about having a spider phobia, being worried that their daughter may be anorexic or that their son may suffer from dyslexia they are referring not to abstract concepts (the *idea* of a phobia, anorexia or dyslexia) but to the presence, perhaps even a material presence in the form of genes or parts of the brain, of a real entity. But phobias, anorexia and dyslexia, commonplace as they now appear to be to us, were not part of common parlance even a generation ago. How did these once unfamiliar ideas become familiar and as real to us as the people and objects in our lives? When new ideas and concepts begin to enter a culture, they are necessarily somewhat abstract and un-defined. In order for people to talk about them and to respond to them meaningfully, they must be made more concrete in people's minds. To do this, Moscovici argues that we simplify the complex idea, and distil it down to a few images that we can easily remember. For example, we may remember the name of a particular person associated with the idea, so that the name of Sigmund Freud 'stands for' psychoanalysis, and Charles Darwin for the theory of evolution. We also use metaphors to help us in simplifying and concretising new ideas, so that the unconscious might be seen as a room in your house that is locked, and the process of evolution might be thought of as like a tree, with limbs producing branches, representing the divisions of families and species of animals.

Once an idea is made simpler and more concrete in this way it becomes possible for people to communicate with each other about it. In turn, this proliferation in talk further contributes to its solidity and reality. Despite the fact that the shape of this now shared and commonly recognised phenomenon (phobia, dyslexia etc.) has been produced by human interaction, it comes to have the appearance of something 'out there', a pre-existing and solid thing that we have just discovered. It has become an object for us. Objectification is therefore the 'materialisation of an abstraction . . . the art of turning a representation into the reality of a repre-sentation, the word for a thing into a thing for the word . . . We have only to compare God to a father and what was invisible instantly becomes visible in our minds as a person to whom we can respond as such' (Moscovici, 1984, p. 38). Where words exist, we assume an object or thing exists which the word stands for and we strive to identify it. Moscovici was especially interested in the way that scientific concepts have passed into common usage, and has particularly studied this in relation to psychoanalytic concepts, which, at the turn of the twentieth century, were completely alien to people. Through anchoring and objectification, notions such as the unconscious/conscious split have been accommodated by earlier representations of involuntary–voluntary and soul–mind, and once the concept became bandied about in everyday life the unconscious became a real object for people, observable and plain to see in the behaviour of themselves and others. In this way, the everyday interactions of people contribute to the metamorphosis of earlier social representations.

This focus upon the psychological processes thought to be involved in the production and reproduction of social represen-tations has understandably made the theory attractive to some social psychologists, particularly those already operating within the field of cognitive social psychology (for example, the study of attributions or attitudes). But one consequence of this is that the theory is open to distortion. If social representations are treated as rather similar to other social psychological concepts, such as attitudes, values or beliefs, they become individualised in the same way and the all-important social dimension of the theory is lost. In fact, one could think of the way that the idea of social repre-sentations gets absorbed into pre-existing and predominant ideas such as 'attitudes' and 'beliefs' as an example of the theory in action! Moscovici was keen to point out that social representa-tions are not just ideas inside people's heads: they have practical implications for us because of the way they are taken up and used by those in positions of power and authority and because of their potential influence on the way we choose to live our lives. For example, current social representations of youth and old age, of gender, of disability or of ethnicity are clearly influential in how we live our lives and in producing the inequalities that exist in society. In this sense social representations are similar to the concept of ideology.

The theory has been criticised on several grounds. Although we should take these criticisms seriously, I would agree with

Augoustinos and Walker (1995) that they should not necessarily lead us to reject the theory. The concept of social representations itself is seen as broad-ranging and rather loosely formulated. It does not lend itself to hypothesis testing, so that the theory is not really falsifiable through research. However, this is also true of other grand theories, such as psychoanalysis, and does not necessarily reflect badly on its analytical power. The theory has also been criticised on the grounds that the supposed consensual nature of social representations does not take account of the diversity of representations in society and the conflicts between them. It appears to suggest that people who share a culture necessarily think in the same way, which is clearly not the case. But this is to distort Moscovici's intention. He certainly did not deny diversity and saw it as one of the reasons why social representations are dynamic, ever changing. Recognising diversity does not mean that there cannot be consensus or similarity between people on some level. It may be argued that, even accounting for the diversity of views among people in the same society, there are ways in which it is meaningful to talk about some aspects of their perspective on the world that are common to, say, a social class, an ethnic group or an age cohort. Of course, there is also the problem that we must then specify how we can talk about the existence of certain groups of people whose social representations we are studying, since the very identification of such groups must (if the theory is correct) in some measure result from our own representations of class, ethnicity, age and so on.

Despite these criticisms, the theory has been taken up and used in a wide variety of research questions, using an equally wide variety of methods. The research methods advocated by Moscovici in order to study the transmission of social representations within society are those of observation in natural settings rather than laboratory experimentation. The aim of such research is to display and examine the world as it is perceived and understood by its inhabitants rather than to search for an objective reality. In fact Farr (1984) is doubtful about the use of laboratory experiments to study social representations because the use of the laboratory itself speaks of a particular social representation of the person that is contradictory to the premises of the theory. Nevertheless, the attractiveness of the theory to a wide range of social scientists has meant that in practice the range of research using the theory as its framework is wide. For example, Herzlich's famous study of representations of health and illness (Herzlich, 1973) used a qualitative, thematic analysis of interview data. She found that people tended to see health and illness as a dichotomy that was mirrored in the dichotomy between the individual and society, with society and its demands being seen as responsible for making us ill and the individual's constitution determining one's power to overcome these. In very different mode, Milgram (1984) studied people's representations of the city of Paris by asking them to draw maps, marking in the landmarks and neighbourhoods with which they were familiar. He found that although the maps were idiosyncratic in many respects, they also showed evidence of being informed by other social artefacts (such as professional maps) and socially shared assumptions about certain areas of the city. Abric (1984), using the laboratory experiment as his research method, investigated the effect of subjects' representations of the situation on their choice of strategy in the 'prisoner's dilemma' game (where two opponents must each choose one of two outcomes from a payoff matrix and try to maximise their profits). The definition of social representation here is taken to refer to the phenomenal reality (rather than objective reality) of the subject – the situation as it *appears* to the person (as earlier recommended by Lewin; see Chapter 1). Abric found that subject's assumptions about the nature of their opponent affected their choice of strategy. The extent to which the representations studied in these various pieces of research can be said to be social clearly varies. But they do share a common concern with the world, *as it is perceived* by the social actor, rather than a desire to reveal an objective reality.

The person, as seen through the eyes of social representations theory, can therefore only be understood in the context of social life. Our perceptions of the world are mediated by social representations, but through our social interactions with others we also contribute to their continuing change and reformulation. We are therefore active agents in the production and reproduction of our social environment. We are not passive products of society, and through our cognitive processes of anchoring and objectification our psychology puts its own spin on the social representations that emerge from our social interactions. The person here is therefore at once both social and psychological.

Discursive psychology

Social representations theory focuses upon the socially shared ideas and images in terms of which people perceive their world, and upon interpersonal interaction. But the theory also has a strong cognitive component, in that it sees these representations as created and reformulated through the processes of thinking, memory and imagination. Discursive psychology shares this focus upon the use of a communally shared stock of ways of talking and upon the importance of interaction, but it takes a radically anti-cognitive stance.

Discursive psychology is a relatively recent, and primarily British, development within social psychology. Its focus of concern is traced back, paradoxically, to a quite traditional and cognitive area of mainstream psychology – that of psycholinguistics. The psychology of language has been dominated by the work of Noam Chomsky in the 1960s. Chomsky's view was revolutionary at the time, offering a radical departure from previous behaviouristic accounts of the acquisition of language. Chomsky claimed that people possess cognitive structures that give them an intuitive grasp of grammar. This means that they are able to create an indefinite number of new, grammatically correct utterances, generated from their intuitive understanding of the rules of language. But Potter and Wetherell (1987) argue that Chomsky chose to study language only through idealised examples of possible utterances, not actual examples of language used by people in interactions. They claim that much of potential interest to the psychologist in the study of language is hidden from view in the traditional study of psycho-linguistics. Indeed, they point out that real examples of everyday language use, with its hesitations, incoherence, repetitive use of common words and phrases and many instances of unconventional grammar do not seem to bear out Chomsky's theory. Language as it is used in common everyday interactions is quite a different matter, they argue, from language as a system of abstract rules.

This suspicion that, in their ignorance of the way language is put to use in practice, psychologists were disregarding a rich source of information was strengthened by other theoretical and methodological influences from diverse sources in philosophy, sociology and linguistics. Potter and Wetherell (1987) draw on the 'speech act' theory of John Austin (1962), the sociological sub-discipline of ethnomethodology and the semiology of Ferdinand de Saussure (1974). Speech act theory points out that much of our daily use of language is not descriptive at all; it does not represent some internal or external state of affairs (such as our thoughts or the state of the weather). Instead it is performative: it accomplishes acts. For example, the words 'I bet you ten dollars that John is late for this meeting' is not a description but an act of placing a bet, and in due course this utterance has practical consequences for the interactants concerned, i.e. the payment of the wager. But language does not have to be explicitly performative in this sense in order to have consequences for speakers, and it is these practical consequences, broadly conceptualised, that are of interest to discursive psychologists. For example, the way that speakers characterise themselves or their part in an event will have implications for other speakers, who may wish to contest the version of events being offered. Ethnomethodology, as practised by sociologists such as Harold Garfinkel (see Chapter 4), provided discourse psychologists with a framework for the study of such discursive interactions. Ethnomethodology literally means the study of the methods (methodology) used by the people (ethno) to produce and make sense of their social lives. Instead of trying to abstract the rules that appear to underlie much of social life, ethnomethodologists were primarily interested in how people put these to use. For ethnomethodologists, people were not so much passive rule-followers as highly competent social entrepreneurs who were capable of creatively drawing on the rules for their own purposes during specific social interactions. In similar vein, discourse psychologists are interested in the way that people construct accounts of themselves and events and in the way that these accounts are carefully crafted for particular purposes. Finally, semiology (the study of how signs and symbols are used in human communication) contributed a concern with the context-bound nature of meaning. The meaning of an utterance does not reside in the words themselves: we have to know something about who is speaking, who they are speaking to and why, and perhaps something of the (at least immediate) history of this particular interaction. Not only this, but the meaning of an utterance is as much given by what is *not* being said as by what is said, so that in order to understand an interaction between people we have to contextualise it and listen for what is absent from it as well as present in it.

Discursive psychologists are concerned with the everyday practice of language use, in the way that people employ the linguistic resources available to them in order to bring off versions of events that have the desired consequences for them. They are therefore interested in examining examples of linguistic exchanges between people, or 'discourse', to find out what goals people are achieving with their talk. But this concern with the performative role of language for people also brings with it important theoretical implications. Language had implicitly been regarded by psychology as an expressive medium, as a way of indicating and communicating to other people what is inside us, our thoughts and our feelings. Even Chomsky's radically new approach to language assumed that utterances were an expression of the grammatical rules that existed as part of the person's cognitive structures. If the things that people say are social acts, governed by the moment-to-moment requirements of social interactions, then they cannot also be simple expressions of internal states. For example, Stearns (1995) points out that our expression of anger is heavily dependent upon the social context: whether it is our partner or boss with whom we are angry, whether we are in a public or private place and the size and nature of the misdemeanour. In a sense, we therefore make a judgement about how angry we should show ourselves to be. Cross-cultural differences in the degree and mode of the expression of anger further suggests that our linguistic expression is not a simple product of an internal state. Thus, our expression of anger is less an outpouring of emotion and more a culturally regulated and normative mode of managing and putting into practice our society's system of rights and obligations – its moral code.

Expressions of anger, and other emotions such as jealousy (see Stenner, 1993) and love, are therefore some of the resources we have for justifying our actions, blaming others, getting our own way and so on; they are tactical moves which have real consequences for us. The same applies to cognitive functions, like memory. Remembering is treated by traditional psychology as 'a kind of distorted re-experiencing, overlaid or altered by subsequent experience and by the machinations of inner cognitive structures and processes, with the report serving merely (and directly) as evidence of those underlying processes' (Edwards and Potter, 1995, p. 35). But of course there can rarely, if ever, be an absolute version of the truth against which accounts may be measured for their accuracy, and much of the 'memory work' performed by people asked to provide an accurate account of an event is directed toward fashioning 'an acceptable, agreed or communicatively successful version of what really happened' (Edwards and Potter, 1995, p. 34).

This is not to deny that people experience emotional states or memories, but these should not be assumed to lie behind our linguistic expression of them in a causal way. Harré and Gillett (1994) point out that only *some* of our bodily feelings and displays are characterised by us as emotions. When we stretch and yawn (an expression of 'feeling tired'), this is not taken by us or by others as the expression of an emotion. They argue that the feelings and expressions we label 'emotions' tend to be the ones where such displays express a judgement and accomplish social acts:

> For example, when one feels or displays envy, this is an expression of the judgement that someone has something that one would oneself like to have. In the case of malign envy, one judges oneself to have been demeaned or depre-

ciated by the possession of that good by the other. To take another example, because a display of anger, irritation or annoyance expresses a judgement of the moral quality of some other person's action, such a display is also an act of protest, directed toward the offending person.

(pp. 146–147)

But we should not mislead ourselves into thinking that expressing a judgement means that we make a (cognitive) judgement, which we then express behaviourally through our emotive conduct. The expression *is* the judgement; it is the form it takes. There is no assumption of cognitive or emotional structures mediating between (internal) feelings or thoughts and (outward) expressions:

> . . . discursive phenomena, for example, acts of remembering, are not manifestations of hidden subjective, psychological phenomena. Sometimes they have subjective counterparts; sometimes they do not. There is no necessary shadow world of mental activity behind discourse in which one is working things out in private.
>
> (Harré and Gillett, 1994, p. 27)

We can begin to see that discursive psychology is a radical departure from traditional North American psychology. The latter has dedicated itself to the study of the internal states (cognitions, emotions, attitudes, beliefs, motivations and so on) of the person, in the belief that these are the cause of the things that people do and say. For example, Edwards and Potter (1995) made an extensive study of transcripts of John Dean's testimony in the Watergate hearings, following that of Neisser (1981). They contest Neisser's view that such transcripts can be used to judge the accuracy of Dean's memory. Instead, they argue that Dean's account of his own efforts to accurately recall events constituted an example of an effective discursive strategy, using appropriate rhetorical devices, aimed at negotiating a credible position for himself:

> Dean's presentation of himself as having a good memory, as being unwilling to take credit that belongs to others, as only following the authority of others, as telling the truth,

all serve to enhance his reliability as a prosecution witness, to bolster his own disputed version of things, and to mitigate his own culpability under cross-examination.

(Edwards and Potter, 1995, p. 19–20)

This study of memory therefore sees the question of the accuracy of Dean's account as, in a sense, unimportant (or at least impossible to determine). What is of interest to the researchers here is *how* Dean constructed his account and made it effective. To the extent that traditional psychology has taken seriously qualitative, language-based data (such as interview transcripts) it has usually viewed these as evidence of and as a route to structures and states existing inside the person, like memories. Discursive psychology thus not only reformulates the role of language in psychology but also considers its usual subject matter, such as internal states and structures, somewhat irrelevant (see Edwards, 1997). In addition, its methodology of choice (discourse analysis) explicitly studies real examples of situated language use, aiming to identify the forms of argument and rhetorical devices being used by the participants. For example, Gill (1993) looked at how male radio broadcasters built accounts which justified the lack of female radio presenters, and Auburn *et al.* (1999) studied police interviews in criminal investigations and showed how disbelief of a suspect's account was constructed and used persuasively by the police interviewer.

But what makes discursive psychology a form of *social* psychology? To answer this we need to return to discursive psychology's particular view of language. Language is of course intrinsically a social phenomenon: it is what enables people in a culture or society to interact and communicate. It is like a common currency; currencies are arbitrary systems but as long as everyone agrees that a pound is made up of a hundred pennies or a dollar of a hundred cents, and as long as there is rough agreement about how much things are worth, then people are able to do business with each other. Currency is therefore a kind of resource for doing business. Language, for discursive psychology, is also a socially available resource. To the extent that we share a common stock of linguistic devices we can go about our business of constructing accounts to fit the purpose at hand. For example, as we grow up and become more sophisticated users of language, we become adept at such rhetorical skills as blaming someone, making an excuse or offering a justification. We come to understand just when to represent ourselves as angry, jealous or wounded, and we come to know exactly how such representations may be constructed. For example, we know that, in our culture, it is assumed that we may sometimes be overcome by powerful feelings, leading us to speak or behave improperly, so that if we wish to justify or excuse our behaviour we may mobilise this representation of emotion in our talk (Stearns, 1995). This common stock of rhetorical devices and representations has been termed 'interpretative repertoires'. 'By interpretative repertoires we mean broadly discernible clusters of terms, descriptions and figures of speech often assembled around metaphors or vivid images . . . They are available resources for making evaluations, constructing factual versions and performing particular actions' (Potter and Wetherell, 1995, p. 89).

Interpretative repertoires may therefore be seen as a shared social resource, a tool-bag of devices and images which a member of a social group can use in fashioning accounts to serve the purposes of the moment. Their use can only be effective so long as members of the social group implicitly agree to use them in accordance with the rules of the game. If we try to use a particular repertoire on the wrong occasion or in the wrong context our account will fail. For example, as we grow up we learn that in our culture people set some store by notions of fairness and equity. We know that representing something as fair (or unfair) can be an effective strategy in getting our point across. Arguing that some people do not have a fair share of the world's resources can encourage people to, say, give to a charity. But the child who tries to mobilise the 'fairness' repertoire by claiming that he or she should be allowed to stay out all night because 'everyone else's parents let them' may not be so successful.

There are therefore some similarities between the theory of social representations and discursive psychology. Both see social interaction as the site where people jointly construct the social resources, the currency that enables them to do business with each other – social representations, or interpretative repertoires in the case of discourse psychology. They are therefore interested in the workings of language in practice rather than as an abstract system of rules, and see the use of such shared resources as a defining feature of social life. In terms of their research methodologies, they share a preference for qualitative forms of analysis of naturally occurring social events. Both are *social* psychologies for these reasons. But they take different views when it comes to the role and status of cognitive processes. While discursive psychology does not deny the existence of processes we might wish to label as 'thought' or 'memory', it does not see these as instrumental in the production or use of interpretative repertoires. Discursive psychology is critical of the theory of social representations for appearing to locate these inside people's heads, which then come to be thought of as lying behind and expressed in social interaction: 'Given the essentially performative and indexical nature of language use how can researchers construe it as a neutral record of secondary phenomena, in this case cognitive or mental states?' (Potter and Wetherell, 1987, p. 145).

This does seem to be a reasonable criticism of social representations theory, which, as mentioned above, has tended to be used in such a way as to equate social representations with previously existing cognitive concepts such as 'attitude' and 'belief'. However, I think the criticism draws attention away from an important and difficult issue that social representations theory tries to address and which discursive psychology largely ignores, and this is the relationship between the social and the psychological. If we are to move beyond the traditional conception of social psychology as the study of how the social environment affects the pre-existing individual (the view espoused by both F.H. Allport and G.W. Allport, see Chapter 1) then we need theories that reconceptualise the individual in social terms. Symbolic interactionism (see Chapters 3 and 4) and social representations theory both try to do this. Discursive psychology goes some way down this road in its conceptualisation of language use as socially

derived and occasioned (rather than as issuing from psychological states) but has not addressed the nature of the person as
repertoire-user. Discursive psychology attempts to empty the
person of any psychological life relevant to an understanding of
language use. But the meaning of a person's talk must then be
taken out of their hands. Mills (1997) criticises discourse analysis
(as it is practised by discursive psychologists) for failing to explicitly address the perspective of the speaker while implicitly equating
it with that of the analyst; the meaning of interactants' talk is
assumed to be transparent to the analyst and its possible interpretation by other parties is not investigated. Furthermore,
discursive psychology implicitly characterises the person as motivated to build socially credible and defensible accounts but does
not explicitly address the psychological status of this. We may
agree with discourse psychology that concepts such as 'motivation', 'drive', 'attitude' and 'belief' are misleading as explanations
of the content and purpose of our talk, but it nevertheless needs
to specify the psychological nature of this discourse-using person,
and the nature of the relationship between that psychology and
the social realm in which it is located. In this sense, it is hard to
see how the discursive approach outlined here can be called a
psychology as such. Social representations theory may indeed
be too traditionally cognitive in its solution, but, like symbolic
interactionism, at least it does attempt to describe how, and with
what consequences, for want of a better phrase, the social gets
inside us.

Social constructionism and critical psychology

Discursive psychology emphasises the constructive work that
people do in building accounts of events. Although it is not explicitly stated in discursive work, this appears to endow the individual
person with a certain degree of agency. It also suggests that the
interactive and conversational work of people may be important
in understanding how ideas, representations and repertoires available to a group or society might become disseminated, adopted,

appropriated and ultimately changed through language use. The body of theory that has in recent times come to be known as social constructionism (see Burr, 1995; Gergen, 1999) emphasises instead the constructive power of language as a system of signs rather than the constructive work of the individual person. I have chosen to treat discursive psychology and social constructionism as separate approaches in this chapter, but should point out that elsewhere (Burr, 1995) I have discussed discursive approaches under the general rubric of social constructionism. Discursive psychology may be thought of as a form of social constructionism, since it emphasises the constructed nature of versions of truth and locates the site of such constructions firmly in the social, inter-personal realm. Since that time, however, the term 'discursive psychology' has emerged and now is used increasingly to refer to research which focuses upon the use of repertoires in the construc-tion of accounts. It therefore seems reasonable here to treat discursive psychology and social constructionism separately.

Social constructionism shares some of its historical and theoretical roots with discursive psychology, particularly in the influence of the work of Saussure. But it takes its philosophical framework primarily from the work of contemporary French philosophers such as the 'deconstructionist' approach of Michel Foucault and Jacques Derrida's ideas about the relationship between our conceptual categories and the 'real' world.

Foucault was originally an historian and was interested in some of the social changes that had come about over the last two or three hundred years. He was especially interested in changes in perceptions of sexuality and mental illness and in the social practices concerning these (Foucault, 1965; 1976). His views were unorthodox, since they challenged the common-sense view that society had progressed toward a more accepting, liberal and humane approach to such matters. Whereas in what we might think of as the bad old days, sex was a taboo subject and the insane were treated like criminals and locked in dreadful asylums, today we uninhibitedly talk about sex and the mentally ill are given therapy. Nevertheless, Foucault argued that these are by no means uncomplicated improvements. Much of our talk about sex and sexuality focuses upon our concerns about what is morally right, normal, perverted or unnatural and those seen as sexually deviant or labelled mentally ill very often are stripped of many of the normal rights and privileges of sane, sexually 'normal' people. Foucault argued that the way people talked about and thought about sexuality and mental illness, amongst other things – in other words the way these things were widely represented in society – was accompanied by implications for the way we treat people. In particular, our representations bring with them particular kinds of power relations. For example, as a society we think of people who behave in a bizarre fashion and hear voices as mentally ill and place them in the hands of psychiatrists and other mental health workers who then have power over many aspects of their lives. Our representations of sexuality as either normal or perverted means that some people's sexual preferences render them sick (and so they join the ranks of the mentally ill) or criminal. The insane do not have political power since they may not vote, and (in the UK) homosexuals may not marry or legally consent to sex at the same age as heterosexuals.

Foucault referred to such representations as 'discourses', since he saw them as constituted by and operating through language and other symbolic systems. Our ways of talking about and representing the world through written texts of all kinds, through pictures and images, all constitute the discourses through which our subjective world is experienced. The world as we know and understand it, therefore, is a world constructed and fashioned according to the discourses circulating in society at any given time in history. Are people who hear voices *really* possessed by demons, visited by angels, conversing with their ancestors or mentally ill? From the perspective of social constructionism, the question is a meaningless one. Any answer to the question is always inevitably a reflection of currently predominant discourses, current versions of what counts as knowledge. The best we can do is to say that people are *constructed as* mentally ill or sane, as sexually normal or perverted. This goes for any other aspect of our identity, such as our gender (our masculinity or femininity) or our age (whether we are old, middle-aged or youthful). The way that discourses construct our experience can be examined by *deconstructing* the texts in which they appear, taking them apart and showing how they work to present us with a particular vision of the world.

Jacques Derrida was keen to point out that language gives us a way of carving up the world into categories, like sane/insane and old/young, but the categories themselves shift and change throughout history, and new ones appear as social circumstances change (for an accessible introduction to Derrida's ideas, see Collins and Mayblin, 2000). For example, the category 'teenager' is a very recent one, and has appeared as young people's status and role in society has changed. Social constructionists therefore maintain that we can have no confidence that the categories embodied in our language bear any relationship to the real world, and indeed that it probably makes no sense to try to make a distinction between the nature of the world as it really is and our constructions of it, since we can never step outside of our language system and see the world in some hypothetically pure state. The social constructionist is therefore deeply suspicious of the positivist's claim to be able to discover the true nature of the social world through scientific enquiry; all we will turn up, they would say, are our socially produced constructions of it.

Some social constructionists want to maintain in their accounts some version of an underlying reality while still approaching traditional psychological and social psychological theories and research with the critical scepticism of social constructionism. This approach has come to be known as critical realism (see Parker, 1997; 1998a). Critical realists are concerned about the possibility that social constructionists might be theoretically unable to challenge some constructions of the world (for example that some races are less intelligent than others) and advocate other constructions (perhaps that differences in attainment are the result of real power inequalities embedded in the structure of society). Social constructionism appears to lead to a position whereby we are unable to say that there are real inequalities between people, only that this is one possible way of looking at the world. There is also the danger that we may be unable to make moral choices, since it can seem as though there is no way of preferring one perspective to any other.

So critical realists prefer to maintain some idea of a bedrock of material and social conditions, such as poverty or inequalities in educational and job opportunities, and the power relations that go with these, in order to be able to advocate political action. Nevertheless, Parker also fears that critical realism may end up being distorted and used against its own intentions: '. . . "realism" of different varieties is already being mobilized by those sympathetic to mainstream psychology to warrant it as a science and to rebut social constructionist critiques . . .' (Parker, 1998a, p. 2). On the other side of the argument, Gergen (1999) celebrates the multiplicity of voices that abound in the world. He argues that, far from neglecting issues of value and ethics, social constructionism guards against the wiping out of oppositional perspectives, the prevailing of one view of what is good and right that is supposed to serve all, while Burkitt (1996) argues that the radical scepticism of social constructionism ensures that any construction of people or events will be subjected to critique and its dangers exposed.

The implications of social constructionism for the person are quite profound. An extreme social constructionist view would see the person as little more than the unwitting product of massive but largely invisible linguistic structures and processes – discourses. We may like to think of ourselves as unique individuals in charge of our own thoughts, opinions and beliefs, but these very concepts (individual, thought, belief etc.) are themselves socially shared constructions, categories built with our language. Our very subjectivity, therefore, our understanding of who we are and our experience of ourselves and others, is a socially constructed artefact. The concept of 'self' is problematised, and is explained away as an illusion produced from our immersion in discourses of the individual and of personality. I think that this extreme social constructionist stance is unnecessarily deterministic, and in the end is as unhelpful to people as other deterministic perspectives. Biological determinism paralyses us because it suggests that we cannot change our nature and must simply learn to live with it, and environmental determinism portrays us as helpless victims of our past formative experiences. However, extreme versions of social constructionism are just as unhelpful

127

because they do not provide any hope that the person can escape the constructive power of language.

But some writers have tried to maintain a broadly social constructionist position while arguing that the person has some room for manoeuvre, some possibility of reflecting upon and challenging the constructions in which they find themselves enmeshed. For example, Carla Willig argues that 'By revealing the constructed nature of psychological phenomena, we create a space for making available alternatives to what has become psychological common sense' (Willig, 1999, p. 2). Parker *et al.* (1995) not only examine and critique the discourses currently constructing persons as mentally ill but also offer alternative constructions in tandem with alternative, and potentially more empowering and facilitative, mental health practices. Some writers (e.g. Hollway, 1984, and Parker, 1992) argue that implicit within discourses are a number of 'subject positions' which persons are silently invited to occupy and which bring with them consequences for how they feel able to speak and behave (subject positions may be thought of as in some ways similar to the concept of role in dramaturgical perspectives – see Chapter 3). Davies and Harré (1990) argue that these subject positions may be thought of as also operating at a more interpersonal level, so that although in the course of social interaction we may be implicitly positioned as a particular kind of person, we are also able to resist the identities we are being cast into by our own skilful use of language.

Social constructionism therefore represents a radical questioning of psychology's and social psychology's assumptions and the knowledge that the disciplines have gathered. From this perspective, far from discovering the truths of human nature, psychology and social psychology have been busily taking part in the social construction of the contemporary modern individual through a massive production and dissemination of discourses, ways of talking about and representing human nature. Through the publication of books and scientific journals, the education of undergraduate and postgraduate students, the proliferation of training in therapy and counselling and the popularisation of psychological matters via the media, psychology has taken a leading role in fashioning human subjectivity as we experience it today. If we think of and experience ourselves as well or poorly motivated, as driven by desires we do not understand, as holding liberal or conservative attitudes, as introverted or extraverted personalities, as intelligent or average, as neurotic or stable and so on ad infinitum, in large measure we have psychology to thank or blame. But not only has psychology been active in bringing into existence the very object of its own study, it has also brought with it some very effective means of censuring, guiding and controlling people. The judgements that psychiatrists and psychologists make about our mental health, our sexuality, our social adjustment, our criminal or alcoholic tendencies, our intelligence, our leadership potential and a whole host of other qualities and dispositions, have real and sometimes far-reaching consequences for how we feel able to or are allowed to live our lives. Foucault (1976) argues that we have become a society so preoccupied with measuring itself against all kinds of psychological norms, so concerned with being normal, that we have effectively become our own disciplinarians. Those in power no longer need to use threat or coercion to keep us in line: we have voluntarily strait-jacketed ourselves, and psychology has helped us to do it.

This line of thinking has contributed to the development of a critique of psychology and social psychology, so that there is now a body of literature referred to as critical psychology and critical social psychology (e.g. Stainton-Rogers *et al.*, 1995; Fox and Prilleltensky, 1997; Ibanez and Iniguez, 1997), and this in some ways can be thought of as the current manifestation of the crisis in social psychology outlined in Chapter 1. Those writing from such a critical perspective have aimed to demonstrate how psychological theory and practice have functioned to marginalise some groups, to misrepresent or distort the experience of others and to silence or disallow the voices of the people who are the subjects of psychological investigations. They aim to show how psychology as a science has never been, and never could be, value-free and that the practice of psychology is unavoidably a political matter. Research carried out from within this framework has quite different aims and often takes a different form from traditional psychological research. Critical, social constructionist research cannot be concerned with the positivist project of discovering truths about human nature, since social constructionism denies the possibility of a final description of people. Instead, it is concerned to analyse the discourses presently constructing us as human beings and to lay bare the historical and social conditions that support these. It is concerned to allow the voices of those researched to be heard and to be properly contextualised, and therefore commonly adopts qualitative methods such as depth interviewing in naturalistic settings, and encourages an active reflectiveness, by the researcher, on their own role in the research process, referred to as 'reflexivity'.

Social constructionist researchers may, like discourse psychologists, use written transcripts of speech as their material for analysis. But they may also search for signs of the operation of discourses in a variety of other sources. Since many physical artefacts carry symbolic meaning for us, it is possible to read them for evidence of discourses, to 'interrogate' them and reveal what they may tell us about who we take ourselves to be. So as well as analysing written texts (which may or may not be transcripts of speech), researchers have looked at materials as diverse as film and TV, gardens and cities (see Parker and the Bolton Discourse Network, 1999).

Summary

The three theoretical perspectives that have been dealt with in this chapter have some degree of commonality. They are all *social* psychologies because each proposes some version of a socially produced and shared set of resources for making sense of the world and, like symbolic interactionism, each emphasises the importance of language in producing, maintaining and changing these meanings. Underpinning their accompanying research strategies is an anti-positivist stance: research is not about uncovering an objective reality but about how representations or versions of the world are constructed and used, and this research preferably takes place in naturalistic settings.

They differ in terms of whether their focus is primarily at the micro level of the individual and interpersonal interaction or at the more macro level of social structure. While social representations and discursive psychology are concerned with the language use of individuals, social constructionism focuses upon discourses as large-scale structures that manifest in the fabric of our texts and other symbolic artefacts. This does not necessarily make these different approaches incompatible, though there has been some debate between discursive psychologists and social constructionists regarding the extent to which each can accommodate the concerns of the other. A more radical difference has to do with the psychological or social status of representations, interpretative repertoires and discourses. While both social representations theory and social constructionism make use of the idea that people experience their worlds in terms of categories of events, for discourse psychologists and social constructionists the strong cognitive flavour of social representations theory is unacceptable. It appears to locate these representations inside people's heads and therefore threatens to bring about a slide back into the individualism that they are trying to escape. Nevertheless, as I pointed out above, social representations theory at least attempts to theorise the relationship between the psychological and the social, a problem which discursive psychologists and social constructionists have, for the most part, not really tackled (but see Burr and Butt, 1999).

A third difference concerns the degree of personal agency allowed by each of these perspectives. Social representations theory is fairly clear about the active role that individual persons play in the transmission and change of social representations. It seems to allow us the capacity to affect how people and events are seen by others through the ways we may choose to use social representations ourselves. Discursive psychologists, although they have not addressed the question of the psychological nature of the discourse-user, do foreground the rhetorical manoeuvres practised by people in their efforts to bring off credible accounts of

THE PERSON IN SOCIAL PSYCHOLOGY

themselves. Social constructionists differ in the extent to which they allow people a degree of agency. Social constructionists who occupy the extreme end of the continuum see the person as an outcome, an end product, of the workings of discourse. In this view it is very hard to see how people might intentionally contribute to change or even manage to reflect upon their own position within discourses. Other social constructionists prefer to see the person as simultaneously constructed by and constructing discourses, and endow the person with the ability to reflect upon and accept or resist subject positions in discourse, although the psychological processes whereby this is possible have rarely been made explicit.

Suggested further reading

Burr, V. (1995) *An introduction to social constructionism.* London: Routledge.

Farr, R.M. and Moscovici, S. (eds) (1984) *Social representations.* Cambridge: Cambridge University Press.

Mills, S. (1997) *Discourse.* London: Routledge.

Chapter 6

The person
in social
psychology

Where's the 'social' in social psychology?

IN THIS BOOK I HAVE DISCUSSED a variety of
perspectives and theories that may be referred
to as social psychology and, in each case, I have
asked what it is about them that is social. The
answers to this question are also very varied, and
have important implications for what can be said
about the central concern of the book and of this
final chapter – the nature of the person in social
psychology. For the purposes of drawing out
the relevant themes I have chosen to contrast the
current individualistic and intrapsychic approach
of social cognition with a variety of others that
may be thought of as interpersonal, societal or a
mixture of both.

The intrapsychic model: social cognition

It may be argued that the predominant psychological social psychology with which psychologists are familiar has become increasingly individualistic and intrapsychic in orientation in recent times. In the past it has often been concerned to identify the impact of the presence or conduct of other people upon the functioning and behaviour of individuals, for example in the social facilitation experiments of Triplett (1898) which are regularly quoted as being among the very first experiments in social psychology. Much research on phenomena such as obedience, conformity, bystander behaviour, group decision-making and interpersonal attraction can be thought of as fitting this picture. The social here is conceived as a set of variables relating to other people and their conduct that may influence a pre-existing, self-contained individual. Other research and theory, particularly that which focuses upon dynamics within and between groups, has sometimes gone beyond this position to suggest that a person's location within social groups is an important source of identity and self-esteem. The role of the social here is not simply one of *impacting* upon a pre-existing individual but in some way helping to *create* that individual. However, developments in psychological social psychology towards the end of the twentieth century have led to an increasingly individualistic position, and one which may be hard to defend as social at all. The rise of cognitive psychology and cognitive science has been mirrored in social psychology. Cognitive theories have been enthusiastically developed in two areas of what has come to be known as 'social cognition', attitudes and attribution, which now occupy central positions in social psychology.

Attitudes used to be thought of as predispositions to respond to a certain object or class of objects (such as President Bush, computers or Italian food) in particular ways. These responses included our thoughts, our emotions and our behaviour. Even here, the concept can be seen to have moved substantially away from the notion of social attitudes used by earlier social psychologists (see Chapter 1). But today the concept of attitude is more likely to be used to refer to our general evaluative stance toward an object, that is the extent to which we see it as good or bad or the extent to which we may be said to like or dislike it. A good deal of contemporary attitude research and theory has focused upon the relationship between attitudes and behaviour, that is whether we can predict a person's behaviour from knowledge of their attitude. By the 1960s and 1970s it was becoming clear that general attitudes (such as a person's political stance or their attitudes toward ethnic groups) were very poor at predicting specific behaviours (Wicker, 1969). We may think of this as cautioning against a view of attitudes as private mental properties. However, the response to these findings led to an even more feverish search for the individual, cognitive processes supposed to underlie the relationship between attitudes and behaviour. Contemporary theories such as the theory of reasoned action (Fishbein and Ajzen, 1975) and the theory of planned behaviour (Ajzen, 1991) argue that behaviour is predictable when we can identify the size or strength of factors such as our attitude toward committing a particular behaviour (for example breast-feeding) and our perception of how this behaviour will be viewed by others. These together give rise to our intention to commit the behaviour, and it is this intention which predicts the behaviour itself. These theories have been used with some success, in particular to predict specific health-related behaviours. But they reduce attitudes to a mathematically weighted combination of properties of the individual that are entirely cognitive in nature.

The same can be said of contemporary attribution theory. Attribution theory concerns the everyday judgements that we make about the causes of events and of behaviour, both the behaviour of others and our own. It is dominated by two theories, those of Jones and Davis (1965) and Kelley (1967). Jones and Davis built on the much earlier work of Fritz Heider (1958) who argued that people behave as naïve scientists who try to make sense of events around them in terms of cause and effect. Jones and Davis proposed the theory of correspondent inferences. According to this theory, we tend to assume that behaviour and events can be explained by, or correspond to, people's intentions and dispositions. But we are also aware that behaviour can be the result of other factors, like social pressures and the desire to look good in front of others. According to this theory, we make a judgement about whether or not a behaviour was due to dispositional factors by processing information about three aspects of it: whether the behaviour is socially desirable, how unusual the chosen course of action or behaviour appears, and whether the action is seen as affecting or intended to affect the perceiver. In his principle of 'covariation', Kelley (1967) argued that people see one event or behaviour as causing another if they are seen to covary, that is whether there is an observable relationship between them. In order to make a judgement about this, Kelley says we use information about three aspects of the event of behaviour: consistency, that is whether a person generally behaves in that way in response to that kind of situation; distinctiveness, whether the person usually behaves in that way across a range of different situations; and consensus, whether most people would tend to respond in that way. The theory predicts that we are most likely to make a dispositional attribution, that is to see the person's disposition or personality as the cause of the behaviour, when consistency is high and when distinctiveness and consensus are both low. Both of these attribution theories lend themselves to laboratory experimentation, where the relevant dimensions of information are manipulated and the effects on attribution are observed, and the person is conceived as following a quasi-mathematical procedure when weighing up the available information.

As Augoustinos and Walker (1995) point out, the information-processing metaphor of the person that is primarily adopted in modern social cognition renders the approach social only in so far as the information processed is about social objects – that is, people (and where the attitude object is not a person or class of persons even this basis is absent). While not dismissing out of hand the contribution made by social cognition, they argue that:

> Currently, research and theory in social cognition is driven
> by an overwhelming individualistic orientation, which forgets

that the contents of cognition originate in social life, in human interaction and communication. The information processing models central to social cognition study cognitive processes at the expense of content and context. As such, societal, collective and symbolic features of human thought are often ignored and forgotten. Contemporary social cognition research is individualistic because it searches within the person for the causes of behaviour. Social cognition will never explain adequately the totality of socio-cognitive experience so long as it remains at the individual level of analysis.

(pp. 3–4)

Interpersonal and societal models: joint action, narrative and positioning

A number of both older and newer approaches share a concern not only to emphasise the social in social psychology but also to re-write the psychological itself as fundamentally socially derived. As we have seen in earlier chapters, even that seemingly axiomatic psychological entity 'the self' may be thought of as emerging from our interactions with others, the social roles we play, the groups we belong or aspire to, and the language and culture we share with others. Symbolic interactionism, role theory and labelling theory all place great importance on our interactions with each other in the development of our selfhood. More recently, a number of psychologists and social psychologists have, in different ways, tried to show how behaviour and selfhood are never the simple outcomes of predispositions or private intentions. Our relationships with others and our interactions with people are instead privileged.

Being yourself is not an uncomplicated matter of acting upon pre-existing personality characteristics in a predictable way. As we saw in Chapter 2, our behaviour is often tied to the specific characteristics of the situations we find ourselves in. But does that mean we are in many cases not being true to ourselves?

Butt *et al.* (1997) used a personal construct methodology to investigate the circumstances in which people felt they could or couldn't be themselves. They interviewed people about how they felt and behaved when they were with each of a number of people with whom they had some kind of relationship. 'Being myself' turned out to be consistent with a wide range of sometimes contrasting behaviours and feelings. Different relationships drew out different kinds of conduct, and in each case the person nevertheless felt that they were being themselves; there was no self that pre-existed their relations with others, rather 'being yourself' is the experience of unselfconsciously 'going with the flow' in interactions. The times when people felt that they could not be themselves were when they felt they had to monitor the interaction and their own behaviour for fear of finding themselves drawn into conduct they would regret or find difficult to handle.

Social behaviour is thus not well characterised as either the outcome of private intentions or as the impact of environmental factors on a pre-existing self. Our interactions with each other certainly involve a coordination of the behaviour of each person but in no way can be thought of as predictable outcomes of pre-existing factors, dispositions or intentions. Our interactions are more like a dance, where we fit our moves to those of the other person. The essence of interaction, like dancing, is not best described as a stimulus–response sequence. Shotter (1993) refers to this as 'joint action', and this term nicely signals the idea that our conduct in interactions is not in any simple way a function of the plans, intentions or dispositions of the individuals taking part. Our conduct arises out of the interaction, and sometimes we find ourselves doing, saying and thinking things that we ourselves find surprising:

> . . . we act just as much 'into' the opportunities and invitations, or 'against' the barriers and restrictions they offer or afford us, as 'out of' any plans or desires of our own. Thus, the stony looks, the nods of agreement, the failures of interest, the asking of questions, these all go towards what it is one feels one can, or cannot, do or say in such situations. This

is joint action; it is a spontaneous, unselfconscious, unknowing (although not unknowledgeable) kind of activity.

(p. 47)

One way of understanding the direction that our interactions and relations with others take comes from the use of narrative (see Gergen and Gergen, 1984; Sarbin, 1986). It is suggested that a fundamental feature of human beings is their propensity for framing their experience within a narrative structure. Quite simply, we make up stories about ourselves, about others and about events in the world. A story has a recognisable structure. It has a beginning, middle and an end and it has a plot. Many life-stories are about overcoming adversity, about progress toward a better way of life, or about a tragic reduction in circumstances. Of course, not only do we tell our stories to each other and to ourselves, we live them out too. We are likely to anticipate future events in terms of the story in which we see ourselves playing the central character, and our conduct will inevitably bear the mark of those anticipations.

But our stories about who we are and how we came to be that person are not simply our own private affair. If your story has a central character (you) it also has a support cast of all the other people in your life whose actions help to make the story credible and liveable. We are therefore all implicated in each other's stories. Our own stories of who we are become inextricably bound up with the roles we play in the stories of those with whom we are in relationship – family members, lovers, friends, neighbours and so on. This can, of course, lead to conflict. For example our own self-narrative may paint a picture of us as saintly, but the role we play in our parent's or partner's narrative may be as 'neglectful' or 'self-interested'. From the narrative perspective, this negative characterisation of us amounts to more than a difference of opinion, it refers to the roles we are implicitly being offered and must accept if others' stories are to work for them, to be liveable. Some disputes between people in relationships are therefore fundamentally about the need that each of us has to have our stories validated and legitimated, and this means that other people must own up to the roles in which they are cast. This way of thinking about the interdependence of people and their stories is, in this aspect, very similar to what is sometimes referred to as the 'systemic' or 'ecological' approach (Bateson, 1972). In the world of natural history, it has become necessary to see each species not as an entity in its own right but as a feature of an ecosystem where each species is part of the conditions of life for other species. In a similar way we can think of each self as entirely dependent upon other selves for its existence and form. This view has been successfully taken up in the field of family therapy. Difficulties that might otherwise be thought of as the properties of individual persons (say an eating disorder) are re-conceptualised as properties of the family system, as it is often found that as the problem individual improves other members of the family or family relations begin to deteriorate. This view of the self as the product of narratives that we negotiate with others therefore shares some of the assumptions of role theory, discussed in Chapter 3. The unit of analysis is not the individual but the relationship between people.

Gergen (1999), writing from a social constructionist perspective, uses the term 'relational selves' to indicate the way in which he wants to foreground not just interpersonal interaction as the site where we construct ourselves and the rest of our worlds but to show how everything we do and are is shot through with the traces of relationships, not just relationships that are current and close to us but also those that are more distant in time and space. Any single interaction rests upon, and gains its sense from, a dense history of other interactions, shared representations, negotiated memories. Drawing on the Russian literary theorist Mikhail Bakhtin, Gergen argues that 'every action manifests our immersion in past relationships, and simultaneously the stamp of the relationship into which we move' (p. 131). The meaning of our conduct can only sensibly be grasped if we see our words, thoughts and actions as always bearing the traces of meanings that arose from other interactions and relationships past and present, and that these in their turn bear even earlier and more distant traces. If we carry on this analysis ad infinitum, we come to the conclusion that there can be absolutely nothing about us that is not constituted in a dense web of interrelationships spanning society and history. Gergen argues that such a conception of the person radically challenges the notion of the self-contained individual of traditional psychology and social psychology. Phrases such as 'I think' and 'I feel' mislead us into believing that thoughts and feelings are properties of persons rather than of relationships and that perhaps we need new ways of talking, different narratives and metaphors that help us signal a more social, relational understanding of the self. Gergen goes so far as to suggest that such a move in our thinking would be beneficial to society: 'Whatever we are, from the present standpoint, is either directly or indirectly with others. There is no fundamental reason to be "self-seeking" or to treat others as instruments of self-gain' (pp. 137–138). However, we do not necessarily have to agree with this view in order to accept the other parts of his argument.

The theoretical approaches that emphasise an interactional and relational basis for the person either implicitly or explicitly see the person as both constructed (through their engagement with the conduct of others) and constructing (to the extent that one's own conduct is part of the construction process). Some social constructionist writers, like Gergen and Shotter, take relationships and interactions between real persons as their focus. Interactions, conversations and dialogue are privileged as the sites where people come into being. In this aspect such forms of social constructionism are social psychologies in the same way that symbolic interactionism, role theory and labelling are social psychologies. But other social constructionists are more concerned with the constructive power of language and other symbolic forms (discourses). They are social psychologists in a stronger (but not necessarily better) sense since the balance of constructive power between the person and discourse is seen as lying with the latter – or at the very least one can say that their prime concern has been with this end of the spectrum. The theoretical term that has come to be used to talk about the person's relation to discourse is 'positioning' (Hollway, 1989; Davies and Harré, 1990; Van Langenhove and Harré, 1994). This term was originally used to refer to subject positions in discourse. It describes how 'individuals are constrained by available discourses because discursive positions pre-exist the individual whose sense of "self" (subjectivity) and range of experience are circumscribed by available discourses' (Willig, 1999, p. 114). Discourses address us as particular kinds of people, and to the extent that in our behaviour and our experience we respond to that address we have taken up the subject positions on offer in those discourses. Gillies (1999) uses the example of addiction discourse to represent the behaviour and experience of people who smoke. This discourse calls such people into the subject position of addict, with the result that those people then come to understand their behaviour and to experience themselves in those terms. The point that many social constructionists want to make about such positioning is that the subjectivities open to us through positions in discourse may be oppressive and leave us little potential for changing our situation. So for example Gillies argues that the discourse of the smoker as addict is disempowering because the possibilities for change and for taking control of one's life seem small.

However, the notion of positioning has also been taken up in a way that acknowledges the active way in which persons endeavour to locate themselves within particular discourses during social interaction. Willig (1999) gives the example of the man accused of rape who may, in his courtroom defence, position himself within a discourse of male sexuality that locates him as a victim of uncontrollable biological urges. In everyday interactions we take up positions vis-à-vis other people which sometimes turn out to be problematic. Within prevailing discourses governing close relationships, one person may take up the position of 'lover' in an interaction, which implicitly calls the other person into a reciprocal position (and all that entails). However, the other may accept this position or reject it, perhaps by striving to position themselves as 'friend'. You might also want to look back at the physiotherapist–patient example of roles used by Davis (1961) (in Chapter 3), and think of this instead as an example of positioning within medical discourse. This use of the concept of positioning recognises both the power of culturally available discourses to frame our experience and constrain our behaviour while allowing room for the person to actively engage with those discourses and put them to use in social situations. When it is used in this way it provides a social psychology that operates along similar principles to social representations theory, where socially shared representations manifest themselves at the level of individual persons but are at the same time manipulated and changed by them. These two theoretical approaches are, however, quite different in other respects, in particular with regard to the cognitive nature of social representations in comparison with the entirely social nature of discourses. Nevertheless, both approaches try in their own way to account for both the societal and psychological sides of the equation.

The relationship between the individual and society

It is clear that the various theoretical perspectives discussed in this book often have radically different implications for how we conceptualise the relationship between the person and society. To properly understand the person in social psychology we must have some appreciation of this relationship, as it is variously understood, and explore the implications of it in each case.

Within the dominant form of social psychology, outlined in Chapter 1, the individual side of the individual–society relation is privileged. There is at least an implicit assumption that the individual exists as an identifiable and coherent unit prior to society. Society is conceived as a set of variables that impact upon and moderate individual functioning. There is an inherent dualism operating here, where the individual and society, although capable of influencing each other, are understood as independent phenomena. The disciplines of psychology and sociology are then regarded as discrete disciplines charged with the task of investigating the individual and society respectively. This dualism in social psychology is consistent with an experimental, laboratory-based methodology where features of the social world are carefully manipulated in order to observe their effects upon the individual.

It is the same methodology, in reverse, as in mainstream psychology, where social factors are carefully eliminated from experimental conditions in order that the individual may be observed in a hypothetically pure state.

One outcome of such dualist thinking is that we become concerned about the autonomy of the person. In theoretical terms, we become embroiled in a debate about agency and determinism. This is a question about the extent to which we have free will. Are our actions freely chosen, or are they the outcome of forces of which we may be unaware? The agency–determinism debate is not confined to the individual–society dichotomy. For example, within mainstream psychology we can find contrasting theoretical positions that accord the individual different degrees of freedom. For humanist psychologists such as Maslow and Rogers, individuals are seen as fundamentally free to choose the path of their future development (if freed from material constraints and the constraints imposed by social conventions). For behaviourists like Watson and Skinner, by contrast, all our behaviour is necessarily determined by reinforcement contingencies present in our (not necessarily social) environment. Yet again, for psychodynamic theorists such as Freud and Klein, our psychology is determined by early relationships and traumas that we cannot escape. But for (mainstream) social psychology the agency–determinism debate manifests itself in the question of the extent to which our behaviour is the outcome of social forces, perhaps social forces invisible to us. It raises a worry about how certain we can be that we are acting rationally, thinking for ourselves and not just acting on herd instinct. The concerns raised by the research on the social psychology of groups, crowd behaviour, obedience and conformity all to some degree map onto the agency–determinism debate.

But we have to remember that the agency–determinism problem in social psychology is itself to some degree contingent upon the individual–society dichotomy. If we can think differently about the individual–society couple, then the agency–determinism question also becomes transformed and, arguably, less problematic. Social constructionist developments in social psychology (see Chapter 5), which explicitly aimed to re-frame the individual as a thoroughly social being, may themselves be unable to escape the agency–determinism dichotomy. If the person is understood as a product of discourse, the individual and self are seen as illusions or at best constructions over which we have little control. Although some writers have tried to argue that the person is as much constructing as constructed, the processes by which this two-way exchange is supposed to occur are not spelled out. There is therefore a tendency for these formulations, by default, to emphasise the formative power of the discourses we inhabit. Social constructionism therefore is in danger of reproducing the same individual–society dualism upon which mainstream social psychology is founded, but this time privileging the social rather than the individual side of the dichotomy.

Paradoxically, it is earlier writers in the symbolic interactionist tradition whose work is seen as foundational to contemporary social constructionist psychology but whose formulations of the individual–society relationship were both fully articulated and avoided dualism. Thirty-five years ago sociologists Peter Berger and Thomas Luckmann wrote *The social construction of reality*. Drawing broadly on symbolic interactionist thinking, they argued that, despite its appearance as an objective and separate entity, the social world is nevertheless constructed by human action and interaction: '. . . despite the objectivity that marks the social world in human experience, it does not thereby acquire an ontological status apart from the human activity that produced it' (Berger and Luckmann, 1966, p. 78). But not only is the social world one that is dependent on and actively constructed by human beings, humans are in their turn thoroughly social animals:

> Solitary human being is being on the animal level (which, of course, man [*sic*] shares with other animals). As soon as one observes phenomena that are specifically human, one enters the realm of the social. Man's specific humanity and his sociality are inextricably intertwined. *Homo sapiens* is always, and in the same measure, *homo socius*.
>
> (p. 69, italics in original)

Berger and Luckmann saw the relation between individual and society as a dialectical one where human beings continually construct the social world, which then acts back upon the individual. Human beings together construct the social world, but they are not free to construct it in any image they choose, because they are born into a social world that has already been constructed in a particular way by their predecessors. This constructed social world then assumes the status of an objective reality for successive generations of people. Berger and Luckmann express this continuous, circular process thus: 'Society is a human product. Society is an objective reality. Man [sic] is a social product' (p. 79, italics in original).

According to Berger and Luckmann, there are three aspects of this circular process whereby human beings construct a social world and are in turn constructed by it. These are externalisation, objectivation and internalisation. The key to this cycle is the basic expressivity of human beings, our capacity for producing objects and symbols that are capable of carrying meaning beyond our immediate time and place. (The use of signs and symbols, both linguistic and other forms of expression, is a fundamental feature of human communication and the study of this is termed 'semiology'.) Berger and Luckmann give the example of a knife, which may come to stand for an aggressive act. The aggressive act is thus in some way invoked by or represented by the object away from the context of real aggressive acts in the here and now. Similarly, our language functions as a system of symbols that allows us to represent events that are not currently happening. Human subjectivity and experience thus enters the public sphere, becomes externalised by us and available or accessible outside of our personal consciousness, to other people.

At the same time, this externalisation is made possible through our capacity to attach meaning to objects and to signs. The knife is an object, but (in the above example) it has also become an objectification of aggression, and as such may then go on to lead a life of its own as a sign, appropriated and used to signify aggressive acts by other people on other occasions. Objectivations are therefore detachable from the here and now, from the original expression of human subjectivity that occasioned their birth. Signs, gestures and words are objectivations too, even though they do not have a concrete, physical nature like knives, because they carry expressive, externalised meanings that are detachable in the same way. It is but a short step from here to the construction of huge, socially shared structures of meaning that appear to exist as objects in their own right, structures that appear to have an existence and an origin outside of our own human activity:

> Language now constructs immense edifices of symbolic representations that appear to tower over the reality of everyday life like gigantic presences from another world. Religion, philosophy, art, and science are the historically most important symbol systems of this kind. To name these is already to say that, despite the maximal detachment from everyday experience that the construction of these systems requires, they can be of very great importance indeed for the reality of everyday life.
>
> (p. 55)

The process of internalisation completes the process, as meanings are passed on to future generations of society through the child's acquisition of language and through socialisation. We become socialised as we come to read objectivated events, arte-facts, words and signs for their meaning, and to understand them in terms of the meanings that our society agrees that they carry. We therefore become able to understand others' talk and actions and to participate in meaningful interaction with other people.

This way of thinking about the relationship between individual and society, as a dialectical process rather than as a conflict between two pre-existing entities, allows us to think of the person as being both agentic (always actively constructing the social world) and constrained by society (to the extent that we must inevitably live our lives within the institutions and frameworks of meaning handed down to us by previous generations). The sociologist Anthony Giddens (1984) offers just such a dialectical approach in his theory of 'structuration'.

147

Understanding the person in social psychology

Throughout this book I have contrasted the vision of the person, as it is depicted in forms of social psychology that are currently dominant within the discipline of psychology, with alternative models that I have argued are, in various ways, more social. I have also argued that these more social models often give us a more adequate understanding of the person. It is now time to overview the major differences to which I have drawn attention and to discuss the implications that these have for how, as social psychologists, we should go about our investigations.

A fundamental assumption underlying the more social accounts I have discussed is that the person cannot be properly understood if we ignore the social context within which experience and conduct take place. If we insist upon regarding the person as a self-contained entity that pre-exists society, we will inevitably have a distorted and partial understanding of who we are. For some of these accounts, the social context is the group or groups to which we belong (or aspire to), for others it is our interpersonal relationships and the everyday interactions in which we take part, and for others again it is the wider cultural representations and linguistic structures from which our talk and thinking derives. Also, if we treat persons as objects, in the sense of regarding them as passive entities with static and definable qualities, we will fail to reach an adequate understanding of why people act as they do. Most of the 'social' perspectives discussed in this book see the person as, in various ways, engaged in a dynamic process in which other people are always implicated. Selfhood, identity and conduct are seen as not fixed or predictable but negotiated, constructed and produced within social contexts. In the case of several perspectives, such as symbolic interactionism, role theory, labelling theory and social constructionism, although there are no essences inside the person dictating experience and behaviour, the person is never entirely self-determining, free to choose their identity. We struggle to negotiate what we can be and how we can conduct ourselves in the context of the social expectations, roles, narratives or discourses in which we find ourselves enmeshed. We are therefore active, reflexive beings who are constantly in the process of producing ourselves, aided and abetted by others in our social world.

This presents us with a new perspective on the question of personal agency, choice and the possibilities for change. If we reject the deterministic idea that people's experience and conduct is the product of essences or cognitive structures inside them or of social factors impinging upon them, neither can we accept that we have complete freedom of choice. Nevertheless, if we abandon determinism as an inappropriate framework for understanding people and replace it with some form of co-production, we can begin to see that who we are and what we do is as much in our own hands as it is in the hands of others. Identity and conduct are open-ended projects and we have some power to influence the direction they take. To the extent that social psychology has often addressed itself to social issues where change may be desirable, for example attitudes toward health behaviours, prejudice and conflict, we need to recognise that such change is unlikely to be achieved by attempting to manipulate cognitive structures or behavioural tendencies conceived as existing inside the person. All such phenomena become relocated in the interpersonal and wider social context, and research programmes aimed at understanding them with a view to planning interventions that are aimed at social change may therefore be in need of a change in focus.

This brings us to the question of how social psychologists should formulate their research questions and carry out their enquiries. We can see how the kinds of questions that social psychology has tended to ask have been formulated in a way that does not recognise the socially contextualised and socially produced nature of the person's experience and behaviour. Questions like 'Does a person's attitudes predict their behaviour?' and 'Under what conditions is helping behaviour elicited?' are framed within a theoretical perspective where the person pre-exists society and is acted upon by external social factors. We need to ask questions that originate in an understanding of the person as socially embedded. Rather, we might ask questions such as 'How is a particular definition of the situation socially produced?' or 'How

149

THE PERSON IN SOCIAL PSYCHOLOGY

can people in an organisation change its culture?' Those who advocate a socially embedded view of the person often also recommend that we make more use of naturalistic research settings and qualitative methods. This seems to make a good deal of sense. If the focus of our enquiries should be on the relationships, social settings and wider cultural processes that produce and give meaning to a person's experience and conduct, then eliminating or artificially reproducing these in the laboratory is a retrograde step. And sociologists and micro-sociologists (some of whom would certainly refer to themselves as social psychologists) have for decades been engaged in research which asks the kinds of questions in which we should be interested, using ethnomethodological approaches, participant and non-participant observation, interviews, diaries and so on to collect their data. Nevertheless, we should not be too quick to condemn or recommend any particular methods per se. It isn't that laboratory experimentation is necessarily a bad idea in social psychology; there will be many good research questions to which it is well suited. But we do have to be careful about the kind of theoretical assumptions that are informing our questions about people.

In order to widen our understanding of what it means to be a social psychologist, then, it seems that we must push back the borders of the discipline as it has grown up within psychology. We must embrace some of the theoretical and methodological approaches that have led a parallel life to it in sociology, perhaps also drawing on some of the thinking and methods from disciplines outside of the social sciences, such as literary criticism and conversation analysis, as some social constructionists and discourse psychologists have done. This does not mean necessarily abandoning or rejecting the work that mainstream social psychologists are doing, and it is likely that for some research purposes, laboratory, ethnographic and discursive methods might usefully complement each other, resembling a more multidisciplinary approach.

Finally, this ultimately means that the kind of education and training that is offered to students of social psychology (and of course psychology too) needs to be re-thought. In the words of Farr (1996):

Moscovici (1988) states that if psychologists are unable to produce forms of social psychology that other social scientists find useful then those social scientists will invent their own forms of social psychology. This, historically, is what has happened . . . It is difficult for social psychologists within psychology, however, to gain an adequate appreciation of the distorting effects of the parent discipline. It is prudent, however, to look for other forms of social psychology that are not subject to the same distorting influence. There is no need for social psychologists to invent new forms of social psychology. They already exist – but they do so in disciplines other than psychology. One needs, merely, to be literate in those other disciplines.

(p. 131)

Glossary

agency   The capacity of the individual to actively and purposely cause effects in the world. This is denied for determinists for whom all actions are, in the final analysis, caused by factors outside the conscious intention of the person.

behaviourism   Psychological theory which holds that the observation and description of overt behaviour are all that is needed to understand human beings. It argues that individual behaviour is determined by factors in the environment, and behaviours are seen as being acquired through the process of learning.

cognitive science   A multidisciplinary approach to studying artificial intelligence and similar phenomena, bringing together psychologists, linguists, information scientists and others.

cognitivism   An approach to the investigation of cognitive processes such as thinking and remembering which assumes that they can be modelled in terms of the transformation of information.

critical social psychology   An approach that challenges many theories and practices common in social psychology, particularly in terms of how they may maintain an unfair status quo.

determinism A style of thinking in which human action and experience are assumed to be directly caused. Thought and action are understood as the lawful outcomes of certain factors, perhaps biological or social, which affect the individual. The individual does not have personal agency.

discourse analysis The study of the socially available resources which individuals employ to make sense of and act in their world. Typically, individuals are assumed to be simply the channels of such resources rather than having any truly personal perspective.

discursive psychology The specific application of discourse analysis to the investigation of speech or text.

double blind A method of controlling bias in experiments. It aims to avoid self-fulfilling prophecies by ensuring that neither the subjects nor the experimenter who carries out the study are aware of the experimental hypothesis.

dualism The view that there are two distinct realms of reality, often the *mental* and the *physical*.

empiricist An approach to knowledge which assumes that all knowledge of the world is learned through information from our senses.

ethnomethodology Method devised by Garfinkel involving the violation of hidden norms in order to reveal their presence.

experiment Observation of a behaviour or phenomenon under conditions that are controlled by the experimenter. It involves the intentional manipulation of independent variables upon one or more dependent variables.

humanistic psychology A view of human beings that sees every person as unique and as possessing an innate potential for positive growth that we can achieve if we develop fully.

ideology A set of ideas and beliefs about the nature of people and society, providing a rationale for how people should be treated and society managed. Ideologies circumscribe our thinking, making it difficult to escape from their influence.

individualism A cultural orientation in which autonomy, independence and self-reliance are highly valued and take precedence over group allegiances.

intra-psychic Intra-psychic explanations locate phenomena inside the person, in their psychological processes.

norms Attitudinal and behavioural uniformities that define group membership and differentiate between groups.

phenomenal world See phenomenology.

phenomenology Broadly, any theory that takes personal experience as fundamental or primary.

positivism The belief that we can only know what we can immediately apprehend. That which exists is what we perceive to exist. Usually linked to an empiricist approach and an uncritical acceptance of scientific method as the route to knowledge.

psychoanalysis A deterministic body of psychological theory focusing upon the role of early experience and unconscious emotions and motivations in producing our behaviour.

qualitative methods Research methods, such as depth interviewing, where the data gathered are semantic, that is they are in the form of meanings or descriptions, rather than numerical.

reference group A group, to which one may not belong, that is psychologically significant for one's behaviour and attitudes.

reflex arc The minimal set of neurones involved in a reflex action, which is a response that occurs automatically without being mediated by the brain.

scientific method Method for studying nature that involves the collecting of data to test hypotheses.

semiology The study of how signs and symbols are used in human communication. Includes the work of Ferdinand de Saussure, Claude Lévi-Strauss and Roland Barthès.

social cognition Cognitive processes and structures that influence and are influenced by social behaviour.

social constructionism The view that people are not determined by internal or external causes, but that they are constructed through the processes of social interaction and through language.

social identity theory Emphasises how membership of social groups influences one's self-concept, and how people often act not as individuals but as members of a particular group.

social representations theory Looks at how shared beliefs develop and are transmitted in social groups and society. These beliefs function to explain reality and justify action.

stereotype An over-simplified, prejudicial and widely shared image of a social group and its members.

symbolic interactionism Theory which sees human behaviour as the outcome of the individual's membership of the social group. Thought, action and identity are mediated by symbols, primarily language.

References

References

Abrams, D. and Hogg, M.A. (eds) (1990) *Social identity theory: constructive and critical advances.*
Hemel Hempstead: Harvester Wheatsheaf.

Abric, J.C. (1984) 'A theoretical and experimental
approach to the study of social representations
in a situation of interaction', in R.M. Farr and
S. Moscovici (eds) *Social representations.*
Cambridge: Cambridge University Press.

Ajzen, I. (1991) 'The theory of planned behaviour',
*Organizational Behaviour and Human Decision
Processing*, 50, 1–33.

Ajzen, I. and Fishbein, M. (1977) 'Attitude–behavior
relations: a theoretical analysis and review of
empirical research', *Psychological Bulletin*, 84,
888–918.

Allport, F.H. (1924) *Social psychology.* Boston:
Houghton Mifflin.

Allport, G.W. (1954) 'The historical background of
modern social psychology', in G. Lindzey (ed)
Handbook of Social Psychology, vol. 1, pp.
3–56. Reading, Mass.: Addison-Wesley.

Armistead, N. (ed.) (1974) *Reconstructing social
psychology.* Harmondsworth: Penguin.

Asch, S.E. (1956) 'Studies of independence and conformity: a minority of one against a unanimous majority', *Psychological Monographs*, 70, no. 9.

Ashworth, P.D. (1979) *Social interaction and consciousness*. Chichester: Wiley.

Ashworth, P.D. (2000). *Psychology and 'human nature'*. Hove: Psychology Press.

Auburn, T., Lea, S. and Drake, S. (1999) ' "It's your opportunity to be truthful": Disbelief, mundane reasoning and the investigation of crime', in C. Willig (ed.) *Applied discourse analysis: social and psychological interventions*. Buckingham: Open University Press.

Augoustinos, M. and Walker, I. (1995) *Social cognition: an integrated introduction*. London: Sage.

Austin, J. (1962) *How to do things with words*. London: Oxford University Press.

Bateson, G. (1972) *Steps to an ecology of mind*. New York: Chandler.

Becker, H.S. (1953) 'Becoming a marihuana user', *American Journal of Sociology*, 59, 235–242.

Becker, H.S. (1963) *Outsiders*. New York: Free Press.

Becker, H.S. (1978) *The mad genius controversy: a study in the sociology of deviance*. Beverly Hills, Calif.: Sage.

Berger, P. and Luckmann, T. (1966) *The social construction of reality*. London: Penguin.

Blumer, H. (1962) 'Society as Symbolic Interaction', in A.M. Rose (ed.) *Human behaviour and social processes: an interactionist approach*. London: Routledge & Kegan Paul.

Borofsky, G., Stollack, G. and Messe, L. (1971) 'Bystander reactions to physical assault: sex differences in reactions to physical assault', *Journal of Experimental Social Psychology*, 7, 313–318.

Brown, H. (1996) 'Themes in experimental research on groups from the 1930s to the 1990s', in M. Wetherell (ed.), *Identities, groups and social issues*. London: Sage in association with Open University Press.

Brown, R. (1988a). 'Intergroup relations', in M. Hewstone, W. Stroebe and G.M. Stephenson (eds) *Introduction to social psychology: a European perspective*. 2nd edition. Oxford: Blackwell.

Brown, R. (1988b) *Group processes: dynamics within and between groups*. Oxford: Blackwell.

Brown, R. (1995) *Prejudice: its social psychology*. Oxford: Blackwell.

Burkitt, I. (1996) 'Relations, communication and power: selves and material contexts in constructionism', paper presented at Social Constructionism, Realism and Discourse conference, Manchester Metropolitan University, April.

Burr, V. (1995) *An introduction to social constructionism*. London: Routledge.

Burr, V. and Butt, T.W. (1999) 'Psychological distress and postmodern thought', in D. Fee (ed.) *Pathology and the postmodern: mental illness as discourse and experience*. London: Sage.

Butt, T.W., Burr, V. and Bell, R. (1997) 'Fragmentation and the sense of self', *Constructivism in the Human Sciences*, 2, 12–29.

Cherry, F. (1995) *The stubborn particulars of social psychology: essays on the research process*. London: Routledge.

Collins, J. and Mayblin, B. (2000) *Introducing Derrida*. Cambridge: Icon Books.

Cooley, H.J. (1902) *Human nature and the social order*. New York: Scribner's.

Davies, B. and Harré, R. (1990) 'Positioning: the discursive production of selves', *Journal for the Theory of Social Behaviour*, 20, 1, 43–63.

Davis, F. (1961) 'Deviance disavowal: the management of strained interaction by the visibly handicapped', *Social Problems*, 9, 120–132.

De Jong, W. (1975) 'Another look at Banuazizi and Movahedi's analysis of the Stanford Prison Experiment', *American Psychologist*, October. Reprinted in D. Krebs (ed.) (1976) *Readings in social psychology: contemporary perspectives*. New York: Harper & Row.

Deutscher, I. (1984) 'Choosing ancestors: some consequences of the selection from intellectual traditions', in R.M. Farr and S. Moscovici (eds) *Social representations*. Cambridge: Cambridge University Press.

Durkheim, E. (1898) 'Representations individuelles et representations collectives', *Revue de Metaphysique et de Morale*, VI, 273–302.

Edwards, D. (1997) *Discourse and cognition*. London: Sage.

Edwards, D. and Potter, J. (1992) *Discursive psychology*. London: Sage.

Edwards, D. and Potter, J. (1995) 'Remembering', in R. Harré and P. Stearns (eds) *Discursive psychology in practice*. London: Sage.

Elms, A.C. (1975) 'The crisis in confidence in social psychology', *American Psychologist*, 30, 967–976.

Farr, R.M. (1984) 'Social representations: their role in the design and execution of laboratory experiments', in R.M. Farr and S. Moscovici (eds) *Social representations*. Cambridge: Cambridge University Press.

Farr, R.M. (1996) *The roots of modern social psychology.* Oxford: Blackwell.

Festinger, L. (1957) *A theory of cognitive dissonance.* Stanford, Calif.: Stanford University Press.

Festinger, L. and Carlsmith, J.M. (1959) 'Cognitive consequences of forced compliance', *Journal of Abnormal and Social Psychology,* 58, 203–210.

Fishbein, M. and Ajzen, I. (1975) *Belief, attitude, intention and behaviour: an introduction to theory and research.* Reading, Mass.: Addison-Wesley.

Flory, E.J. (2000) URL http://www.oredenet.org/%7ejflory/204s_int.htm

Foucault, M. (1965) *Madness and civilization: a history of insanity in the Age of Reason.* New York: Vintage.

Foucault, M. (1976) *The History of Sexuality,* Vol. 1. Harmondsworth: Penguin.

Fox, D. and Prilleltensky, I. (1997) *Critical psychology: an introduction.* London: Sage.

Gergen, K.J. (1972) 'Multiple identity', *Psychology Today,* 5, 31–35. Reprinted in D.N. Harlow and J.J. Hanks (eds) (1974) *Organizational behavior: concepts and cases.* New York: Little Brown.

Gergen, K.J. (1973) 'Social psychology as history', *Journal of Personality and Social Psychology,* 26, 309–320.

Gergen, K.J. (1999) *An invitation to social construction.* London: Sage.

Gergen, K.J. and Gergen, M. (1984) 'The social construction of narrative accounts', in K.J. Gergen and M.M. Gergen (eds) *Historical Social Psychology.* Hillsdale, NJ: Erlbaum.

Giddens, A. (1984) *The constitution of society.* Cambridge: Polity Press.

Gill, R. (1993) 'Justifying injustice: broadcasters' accounts of inequality in radio', in E. Burman and I. Parker (eds) *Discourse analytic research: repertoires and readings of texts in action.* London: Routledge.

Gillies, V. (1999) 'An analysis of the discursive positions of women smokers: implications for practical interventions', in C. Willig (ed.), *Applied discourse analysis: social and psychological interventions.* Buckingham: Open University Press.

Goffman, E. (1959) *The presentation of self in everyday life.* Harmondsworth: Allen Lane.

Goffman, E. (1961) *Encounters: two studies in the sociology of interaction.* Indianapolis: Bobbs-Merrill.

Goffman, E. (1967) *Interaction ritual: essays on face-to-face behaviour.* Harmondsworth: Penguin.

Goldstein, B. (1959) 'The perspective of unionized professionals', *Social Forces*, 37, 323–327.

Graumann, C.F. (1988) 'Introduction to a history of social psychology', in M. Hewstone, W. Stroebe, J.P. Codol and G.M. Stephenson (eds) *Introduction to social psychology.* Oxford: Blackwell.

Haney, C., Banks, W.C. and Zimbardo, P.G. (1973) 'Interpersonal dynamics in a simulated prison', *International Journal of Criminology and Penology*, 1, 69–97.

Harré, R. and Gillett, G. (1994) *The discursive mind.* London: Sage.

Hartley, R. (1986) 'Imagine you're clever', *Journal of Child Psychology and Psychiatry*, 27, 3, 383–398.

Hartshorne, H. and May, M.S. (1928–1930) *Moral studies in the nature of character: studies in the nature of character.* New York: Macmillan.

Hayes, N. (1994) *Foundations of psychology: an introductory text.* London: Routledge.

Heider, F. (1958) *The psychology of interpersonal relations.* New York: Wiley.

Herzlich, C. (1973) *Health and illness: a social psychological analysis.* London: Academic Press.

Hewitt, J.P. (1988) *Self and society.* Newton, Mass.: Allyn & Bacon.

Hewstone, M., Stroebe, W., Godol, J.P. and Stephenson, G.M. (eds) (1988) *Introduction to social psychology.* Oxford: Blackwell.

Hofling, C.K., Brotzman, E., Dalrymple, S., Graves, N. and Pierce, C.M. (1966) 'An experimental study in nurse–physician relationships', *Journal of Nervous and Mental Disease*, 143, 171–180.

Hollway, W. (1984) 'Gender difference and the production of subjectivity', in J. Henriques, W. Hollway, C. Urwin, C. Venn and V. Walkerdine (eds) *Changing the subject: psychology, social regulation and subjectivity.* London: Methuen.

Hollway, W. (1989) *Subjectivity and method in psychology.* London: Sage.

Hood, W.R. and Sherif, M. (1962) 'Verbal report and judgement of an unstructured stimulus', *Journal of Psychology*, 54, 121–130.

Hyman, H.H. (1942) 'The psychology of status', *Archives of Psychology*, 38, no. 15.

Ibanez, T. and Iniguez, L. (1997) *Critical social psychology.* London: Sage.

Jackson, J.M. (1988) *Social psychology: an integrative orientation.* Hillsdale, NJ: Erlbaum.

Jones, E.E. and Davis, K.E. (1965) 'From acts to dispositions: the attribution process in person perception', in L. Berkowitz (ed.) *Advances in Experimental Social Psychology,* Vol. 2. New York: Academic Press.

Kaye, K. (1982) *The mental and social life of babies.* Brighton: Harvester.

Kelley, H.H. (1967) 'Attribution theory in social psychology', in D. Levin (ed.) *Nebraska Symposium on Motivation,* 15, 192–238. Lincoln, NE: University of Nebraska Press.

Kelly, G. (1955) *The psychology of personal constructs.* New York: W.W. Norton.

Lalljee, M. (1996) 'The interpreting self: an experimentalist perspective', in R. Stevens (ed.) *Understanding the self.* Milton Keynes: Open University Press.

La Pière, R.T. (1934) 'Attitudes versus actions', *Social Forces,* 13, 230–277.

Larsen, K. (1974) 'Conformity in the Asch experiment', *Journal of Social Psychology,* 94, 303–304.

Latané, B. and Darley, J.M. (1968) 'When will people help in a crisis?', *Psychology Today,* September. Reprinted in D. Krebs (ed.) (1976) *Readings in social psychology: contemporary perspectives.* New York: Harper & Row.

Latané, B. and Darley, J.M. (1969) 'Bystander "apathy"', *American Scientist,* 57, 244–268.

Le Bon, G. (1895) *Psychologie des foules.* Paris: Alcan (English translation (1903) *The crowd.* London: Unwin).

Linton, R. (1945) *The cultural background of personality.* New York: Appleton-Century-Crofts.

Maslach, C. (1997) *The Stanford Prison experiment: still powerful after all these years.* URL http://www2.stanford.edu/dept/news/relaged/970108prisonexp.html

McDougall, W. (1920) *The group mind: a sketch of the principles of collective psychology with some attempt to apply then to the interpretation of national life and character.* Cambridge: Cambridge University Press.

Mead, G.H. (1934) *Mind, self and society.* Chicago: Chicago University Press.

Mead, G.H. (1956) 'Self and other', in A. Strauss (ed.) *The social psychology of George Herbert Mead.* Chicago: University of Chicago Press.

George's Page: the Mead Project website. URL http://paradigm.soci. brocku.ca/~lward/default.html

Merton, R.K. (1948) 'The self-fulfilling prophecy', *Antioch Review*, 8, 193–210.

Meyer, P. (1972) 'If Hitler asked you to electrocute a stranger, would you? Probably', *Esquire*, February. Reprinted in D. Krebs (ed.) (1976) *Readings in social psychology: contemporary perspectives.* New York: Harper & Row.

Milgram, S. (1963) 'Behavioral study of obedience', *Journal of Abnormal and Social Psychology*, 67, 4, 371–378. Reprinted in S. Fein and S. Spencer (eds) *Readings in social psychology: the art and science of research.* Boston, Mass.: Houghton Mifflin.

Milgram, S. (1974) *Obedience to authority.* New York: Harper & Row.

Milgram, S. (1984) 'Cities as social representations', in R.M. Farr and S. Moscovici (eds) *Social representations.* Cambridge: Cambridge University Press.

Mills, S. (1997) *Discourse.* London: Routledge.

Minard, R.D. (1952) 'Race relationships in the Pocahontas coal field', *Journal of Social Issues*, 8, 29–44.

Mischel, W. (1968) *Personality and assessment.* New York: Wiley.

Moghaddam, F.M., Taylor, D.M. and Wright, S.C. (1993) *Social psychology in cross-cultural perspective.* New York: W.H. Freeman.

Moscovici, S. (1984) 'The phenomenon of social representation', in R.M. Farr and S. Moscovici (eds) *Social representations.* Cambridge: Cambridge University Press.

Moscovici, S. (1988) *La Machine à faire des dieux sociologie et psychologie.* Paris: Fayard.

Moscovici, S., Lage, E. and Naffrechoux, M. (1969) 'Influence of a consistent minority on the responses of a majority in a color perception task', *Sociometry*, 32, 365–380. Reprinted in M. Hewstone, A.S.R. Manstead and W. Stroebe (eds) (1997) *The Blackwell reader in social psychology.* Oxford: Blackwell.

Neisser, U. (1981) 'John Dean's memory: a case study', *Cognition*, 9, 1–22.

Newcombe, T.M. (1951) 'Social psychological theory: integrating individual and social approaches', in J.H. Rohrer and M. Sherif (eds) *Social psychology at the crossroads.* New York: Harper.

Nicholson, N., Cole, S.G. and Rocklin, T. (1985) 'Conformity in the Asch situation: A comparison between contemporary British and US university students', *British Journal of Social Psychology*, 24, 59–63.

Orne, M.T. (1962) 'On the social psychology of the psychological experiment: with particular reference to demand characteristics and their
implications', *American Psychologist*, 17, 776–783.

Orne, M.T. (1971) 'The simulation of hypnosis: why, how and what it
means', *International Journal of Clinical and Experimental
Hypnosis*, 19, 183–210.

Orne, M.T. and Evans, F.J. (1965) 'Social control in the psychological
experiment: antisocial behaviour and hypnosis', *Journal of Personality and Social Psychology*, 1, 189–200.

Parker, I. (1989) *The crisis in modern social psychology – and how to
end it.* London: Routledge.

Parker, I. (1992) *Discourse dynamics: critical analysis for social and individual psychology.* London: Routledge.

Parker, I. (1997) 'Discursive psychology', in D. Fox and I. Prilleltensky
(eds) *Critical psychology: an introduction.* London: Sage.

Parker, I. (1998a) 'Realism, relativism and critique in psychology', in I.
Parker (ed.) *Social constructionism, discourse and realism.* London:
Sage.

Parker, I. (ed.) (1998b) *Social constructionism, discourse and realism.*
London: Sage.

Parker, I., Georgaca, E., Harper, D., McLaughlin, T. and Stowell-Smith,
M. (1995) *Deconstructing psychopathology.* London: Sage.

Parker, I. and the Bolton Discourse Network (1999) *Critical textwork:
an introduction to varieties of discourse and analysis.* Buckingham:
Open University Press.

Perrin, S. and Spencer, C. (1981) 'Independence or conformity in the
Asch experiment as a reflection of cultural and situational factors'
British Journal of Social Psychology, 20, 205–209.

Potter, J. (1996) *Representing reality: discourse, rhetoric and social
construction.* London: Sage.

Potter, J. and Wetherell, M. (1987) *Discourse and social psychology:
beyond attitudes and behaviour.* London: Sage.

Potter, J. and Wetherell, M. (1995) 'Discourse *analysis*', in J.A. Smith,
R. Harré and L. Van Langenhove (eds) *Rethinking methods in
psychology.* London: Sage.

Radley, A. (1991) *In social relationships.* Buckingham: Open University
Press.

Reicher, S.D. (1984) 'The St Pauls riot: an explanation of the limits of
crowd action in terms of a social identity model', *European Journal
of Social Psychology*, 14, 1–21.

Rosenhan, R. (1973) 'On being sane in insane places', *Science*, 179, 250–258.

Rosenthal, R. and Jacobson, L.F. (1968a) 'Teacher expectations for the disadvantaged', *Scientific American*, 218, 4.

Rosenthal, R. and Jacobson, L.F. (1968b) *Pygmalion in the classroom: teacher expectations and pupil intellectual development*. New York: Holt, Rinehart & Winston.

Salmon, P. (1998) *Life at school*. London: Constable.

Sarbin, T.R. (ed.) (1986) *Narrative psychology: the storied nature of human conduct*. New York: Praeger.

Saussure, F. de (1974) *Course in general linguistics*. London: Fontana.

Schaffer, H.R. (1977) *Mothering*. London: Open Books.

Scheff, T.J. (1969) 'The role of the mentally ill and the dynamics of mental disorder: a research framework', in S. Dinitz, R.R. Dynes and A.C. Clarke (eds) *Deviance: studies in the process of stigmatization and societal reaction*. London: Oxford University Press.

Sherif, M. (1935) 'A study of some social factors in perception', *Archives of Psychology*, 27, no. 187.

Sherif, M., Harvey, O.J., White, B.J., Hood, W.R. and Sherif, C.W. (1961) *Intergroup conflict and co-operation: the robbers' cave experiment*. Norman, Okla.: University of Oklahoma Press.

Shibutani, T. (1955) 'Reference groups as perspective', *American Journal of Sociology*, 60, 562–569.

Shibutani, T. (1962) 'Reference groups and social control', in A.M. Rose (ed.) *Human behaviour and social processes: an interactionist approach*. London: Routledge & Kegan Paul.

Shotland, R.L and Straw, M.K. (1976) 'Bystander response to an assault: when a man attacks a woman', *Journal of Personality and Social Psychology*, 34, 990–999.

Shotter, J. (1993) *Cultural politics of everyday life*. Buckingham: Open University Press.

Snyder, M., Tanke, E.D. and Berscheid, E. (1977) 'Social perception and interpersonal behaviour: on the self-fulfilling nature of social stereotypes', *Journal of Personality and Social Psychology*, 35, 656–666.

Stainton Rogers, R., Stenner, P., Gleeson, K. and Stainton Rogers, W. (1995) *Social psychology: a critical agenda*. Cambridge: Polity Press.

Stearns, P. (1995) 'Emotions', in R. Harré and P. Stearns (eds) *Discursive psychology in practice*. London: Sage.

Stenner, P. (1993) 'Discoursing jealousy', in E. Burman and I. Parker (eds) *Discourse analytic research: repertoires and readings of texts in action*. London: Routledge

Tajfel, H., Billig, M.G., Bundy, R.P. and Flament, C. (1971) 'Social categorisation and intergroup behaviour', *European Journal of Social Psychology*, 1, 149–178.

Tajfel, H. and Turner, J.C. (1979) 'The social identity theory of intergroup relations', in S. Worchel and W.G. Austin (eds) *Psychology of intergroup relations*. Monterey, Calif.: Brooks/Cole.

Triplett, N. (1898) 'Dynamogenic factors in pacemaking and competition', *American Journal of Psychology*, 9, 507–533.

Turner, R.H. (1962) 'Role-taking: process versus conformity', in A.M. Rose (ed.) *Human Behaviour and Social Processes: An interactionist approach*. London: Routledge and Kegan Paul.

Van Avermaet (1988) 'Social influence in small groups', in M. Hewstone, W. Stroebe, J.P. Codol, and G.M. Stephenson (eds) *Introduction to social psychology*. Oxford: Blackwell.

Van Langenhove, L. and Harré, R. (1994) 'Cultural stereotypes and positioning theory', *Journal for the Theory of Social Behaviour*, 24, 4, 359–372.

Wicker, A.W. (1969) 'Attitudes versus actions: the relationship of verbal and overt behavioral responses to attitude objects', *Journal of Social Issues*, 25, 41–78.

Willig, C. (ed.) (1999) *Applied discourse analysis: social and psychological interventions*. Buckingham: Open University Press.

Zimbardo, P.G. (1969) 'The human choice: individuation, reason and order versus deindividuation, impulse and chaos', in W.J. Arnold and D. Levine (eds) *Nebraska symposium on motivation 17*. Lincoln, Nebraska: University of Nebraska Press.

Zimbardo, P.G. (1975) 'Pathology of *imprisonment*', *American Psychologist*, October. Reprinted in D. Krebs (ed.) (1976) *Readings in social psychology: contemporary perspectives*. New York: Harper & Row.

Index